I0605384

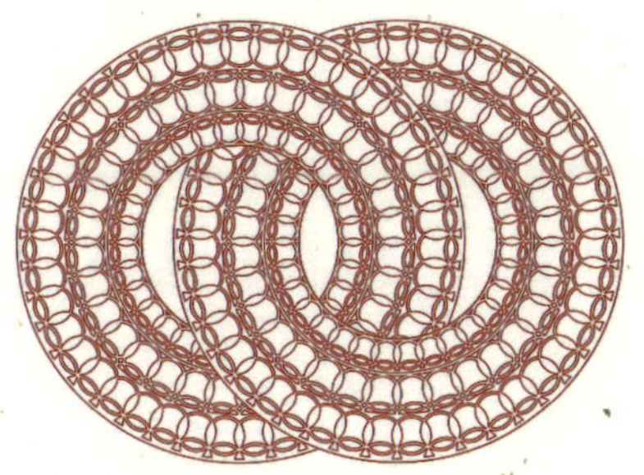

LIGHTS IN COLD ROOMS

LIGHTS IN COLD ROOMS

A Psychologist Reflects
on Family, Aging, Love & Loss

JOAN CUSACK HANDLER, PhD

CAVANKERRY
PRESS

CavanKerry Press Ltd.
Fort Lee, New Jersey
www.cavankerrypress.org

Publisher's Cataloging-in-Publication Data
provided by Five Rainbows Cataloging Services

Names: Handler, Joan Cusack, 1941- author.
Title: Lights in cold rooms : a psychologist reflects on family, aging, love & loss / Joan Cusack Handler.
Description: Fort Lee, NJ : CavanKerry Press, 2025.
Identifiers: ISBN 978-1-960327-15-4 (paperback) | ISBN 978-1-960327-16-1 (ebook)
Subjects: LCSH: Women authors--Biography. | Autobiography. | Psychotherapy. | Grief. | Families—Biography. | COVID-19 Pandemic, 2020-2023--Social aspects. | BISAC: BIOGRAPHY & AUTOBIOGRAPHY / Women. | BIOGRAPHY & AUTOBIOGRAPHY / Memoirs. | FAMILY & RELATIONSHIPS / Death, Grief, Bereavement.
Classification: LCC PS3608.A7 A3 2025 (print) | LCC PS3608.A7 (ebook) | DDC 811/.6--dc23.

Cover artwork: Mike Corrao
Cover and interior text design by Mike Corrao
Editors: Jan Freeman, Molly Peacock, and Baron Wormser
Copy Editors: Bridget Reaume and Joy Arbor
First Edition 2025, Printed in the United States of America

Notable Voices Series

CavanKerry Press is proud to publish the works of established poets of merit and distinction.

Made possible by funds from the New Jersey State Council on the Arts, a partner agency of the National Endowment for the Arts.

NATIONAL ENDOWMENT for the ARTS
arts.gov

CavanKerry Press is grateful for the generous support it has received from the New Jersey State Council on the Arts, as well as the following funders:

The Academy of American Poets
Bergen County Arts
Community of Literary Magazines and Presses
National Book Foundation
New Jersey Arts and Culture Renewal Fund
New Jersey Council for the Humanities
New Jersey Cultural Trust
New Jersey Economic Development Authority
The Poetry Foundation

ALSO BY JOAN CUSACK HANDLER

MEMOIR

Confessions of Joan the Tall

POETRY

GlOrious

The Red Canoe: Love in Its Making

Orphans

ANTHOLOGIES

Breath of Parted Lips: Voices from the Robert Frost Place, Volume 1

The Waiting Room Reader, Volume 1

Places We Return To, coedited with Gabriel Cleveland

For my sister, Catherine Cusack Breitfeller
& my mother, Mary O'Connor Cusack

For my husband, Alan,
our son, David,
& his two daughters,
Cassidy & Elodie,
our miracle granddaughters

CONTENTS

III. *A House Divided Against Itself*

IV. *Banquets & Cameos*

V. *Keep Them Close*

Coda

PREFACE

Depression & the Stories That Came with It

As the world shut down in 2020, a deeper struggle emerged for aging women. Incidents of depression quadrupled among aging women during the COVID pandemic and quarantine isolation. However, psychotherapy, the typical and preferred care in treating depression, was unavailable. Clinicians were not seeing patients. Those who were suffering were left to face their demons alone.

Because I had recently retired from my psychotherapy practice, the quarantine did not affect me professionally, but it did personally. I was among the many thousands of women battling my mental health. I recognized early on that I was slipping into a depression that no longer responded to my antidepressant medication. While confronting any mental or physical illness is frightening, depression's paralyzing nature strips us of hope—the dive into despondence all-consuming. Unable to find a therapist for myself, I was forced to monitor the illness on my own. As a psychologist with a forty-year practice, I understood what was happening to me, and I was terrified.

Depression is a debilitating mental illness identified by a sense of hopelessness; emotional disconnection from family, friends, and events in one's life; excessive sleep or the lack thereof; poor appetite; and little-to-no energy. Incidents can be mild to acute and can occur once or multiple times in a lifetime. In addition to psychotherapy, or talk therapy, treatment often includes medication. But in these textbook descriptions lies an unrelenting weight that can't be so easily described. A silent thief, stealing what makes you *you*.

I've battled with depression all my life. During my most extreme episodes, I felt myself being sucked into a black hole. My worst experience was when I was in my early forties; I remember looking at my son, whom I adore, and felt nothing. There was only darkness. And more darkness. Over four decades, depression periodically stole my life and loves. The loneliness was unbearable.

Sadly, those experiencing depression are often chastised as lazy or weak—*Snap out of it! Pick yourself up by your bootstraps*—as if the illness is under their control, but nothing about depression is controllable. The sense of alienation is intensified by the judgment and lack of empathy expressed by the people around them.

The culprit is a chemical imbalance in the body that precipitates the depression. The body produces and requires the production of certain chemicals called neurotransmitters (dopamine, serotonin, and norepinephrine) to maintain mood balance. However, a set amount of these is produced without accommodation for stress levels. During particularly difficult times, the number of neurotransmitters are actually depleted, causing deeper depressive symptoms. Antidepressant medication augments psychotherapy sessions by providing the body with the chemicals it is missing. For this reason, I sought the aid of a psychopharmacologist, who included medication in my treatment plan to help control my depressive episodes.

In the early days of my pandemic depression, as my mood began to darken and ruminations erupted, I wrote my observations and emotions on whatever envelope, scrap of paper, or napkin was available. Eventually, I switched to filling a notebook, and as the words accelerated, I moved to my computer, where I started a detailed account of my feelings and thoughts. I accepted whatever language and description first came to me. No edits were permitted; the first words that come to us are often the most accurate indicator of unconscious material. Sometimes my writing evolved into a poem or paragraph of poetic prose. Sometimes not. Sometimes they were simply thoughts on paper with no rhythm and no structure. This stream-of-consciousness writing resembled the process of psychotherapy, as the therapist waits for the patient to start speaking and accepts whatever course the patient takes. Oftentimes, in writing and in therapy, the order of events and observations seems random, not linear or even logical on a conscious level. This is how the unconscious reveals itself. And it's the unconscious that holds our truth, history, and emotions, as well as our pain and losses.

This unveiling began the process of solving the puzzle of my depression. To know what lurks inside us is to gain the ammunition to face it—and the spark to ignite change. In psychotherapy, often called "the talking cure," the patient and therapist work together to uncover these insights. During the pandemic, without a therapist to confide in, I turned to the writings in my notebook and on my computer as a form of unfiltered, self-guided therapy.

The exploration, presented in the following pages, is an amalgam of the creative, spiritual, psychological, and real-life circumstances that formed the person that I am today, at eighty. It also revealed the events and emotions that shaped my life, from early childhood to today. During the course of writing and compiling this collection of meditations, I opened myself to the conflicting forces of God, the Church, family, the body, and ultimately, aging. By the conclusion of this memoir—both in writing and the final binding of each book—I achieved a new, evolving awareness and peace. Woven through these pages are poems that give voice to the emotional terrain I navigated. Stories appear of my relationships with my brothers and their separation from the family; my sister's prolonged illness; and the emotional triangle of my mother, my sister, and myself, all so different, yet connected through our love for each other. Also included is the mythic account of my mother, the emotional center of our family; events of her early life in Ireland; and occasions that shaped her as a mother arrested between love and loss. Finally, the book reflects the logic of my unconscious rather than offering accounts in a linear frame.

At the end of it all, I do not recommend self-analysis as a substitute for talk therapy, but I offer it to you as the alternative that helped me when traditional psychotherapy was not possible. The process of free writing is a valuable tool for all of us, whether or not we're in talk therapy. And the decision to share reflections is up to each person. For me, the process of writing increased my awareness of my unconscious life and brought me closer to self-knowledge and peace.

I hope you find it helpful.

Sincerely,
Joan Cusack Handler, PhD
Licensed Psychologist

Patient Clinician

Lately, it's mid to late afternoon before she washes her face and brushes her teeth.
Lethargy, no appetite, endless sleep.
Diagnosis: Clinical Depression.

Multiple triggers: death of her sister,
COVID paralyzing life,
guns, violence, hate.
At the apex, her failing body.

Psychotherapy prescribed,
but her therapist's deceased.
Others quarantined, not seeing patients.

Her problem, she states, is that she's old.
But she doesn't know how to be old.

She's learned how to be successful, sexy, loving,
how to be pregnant, to parent.
Even how to be beautiful. Counsel is abundant.

But no one teaches her
how to know when she's old.

All she sees are the years rushing and her tripping trying to catch up.
Fell three times last year.
It's one of the hazards of aging and facing decline.
I am the patient, and I am the doctor assigned to heal myself.

1

The Body, the Culprit

THE WORST DAY

1952

MY BATTLE WITH MY BODY BEGAN IN EARLY CHILDHOOD, WHEN I noticed I was different from the other kids. Always in a rush, my legs seemed to fly out from under me, leaping many inches off the graph for what was normal for a girl my age. The worst day of my life was the first day of sixth grade, when Sister Mary Lucille announced that we were going to be measured and weighed. My weight didn't bother me—I was quite thin—but my height terrified me.

My belly boiled, and sweat poured down my neck and chest. I jumped up from my desk, blurting out, "I need to go to the girl's room, Sister," and ran out of the room.

It took forever for my breath to slow enough for me to walk shakily back to the classroom.

"Joan, dear, we've reached the last of the C's, so it's your turn," Sister said.

I don't know how I walked to the front. My vision tunneled, and my whole body was trembling.

Sister's voice sang out, "Nice and straight, dear," while she gently pinned my shoulders back and announced in the loudest voice I'd ever heard, "Joan Cusack, five feet, eleven-and-a-half inches."

I was eleven years old.

LOOMING

1950–1960

"Jolly Green Giant! Beanstalk! Stretch!" I was the butt of every bully's joke as I walked to school or the store. I especially hated trips to the grocers, and in a family of six, there were many, always in the afternoon between school and supper. The boys lurked, particularly in the alleyways between the rows of houses, on the lookout for someone to laugh at and torture. My brother Sonny, a year older than me, was often with them. My nemesis all my young life, his favorite taunts were switching off the lights in the cellar when he knew I was down there folding laundry, putting the Cheerios box between us during breakfast so he didn't have to see my face, and laughing at my small breasts, hollering "Carpenter's dream, flat as a board!" and "Two peas on an ironing board!"

As I approached the alley between the two corner houses, the loudest boy would call out, "Hey, Stretch! How's the weather up there?" followed by the rest of the pack chanting, "Yeah, how's the weather up there?"

Most days I just walked straight ahead as if I didn't even hear them. But sometimes, I struck back, gathering my courage and calling, "Just fine!" I loved those moments. I felt strong and unafraid. Even when I was scared that I was, indeed, a giant who would never stop growing, I refused to stoop over to reduce my height. Though my belly scalded with shame, I pretended I didn't hear the insults and walked straighter, with conviction that spelled *pride* to the youngest neighborhood kids who watched from their yards.

I NEVER LET ANYONE KNOW HOW EMBARRASSED I FELT—EVEN MY mother, though she clearly surmised that I was being tortured again. She insisted that the boys were jealous of me and my height was something to be proud of. I knew that wasn't true and though I tried to tell her, she was relentless. Sonny continued to torment me, but I said nothing. Our older sister, Catherine, also hated being tall. She was four years older and three inches shorter, and she'd probably already reached her full height. I couldn't understand why she complained about her height to me. It felt mean. But I remained silent, saying nothing to my girlfriends, parents, teachers. No one knew how I felt. At times, even me.

I envy the nomad—
moving further & further
from home.

My family lived in a tiny working-class community called Edgewater Park in Throggs Neck, the Bronx, on the Long Island Sound. When my parents first moved in, the houses were small summer bungalows. Gradually, the neighborhood brigade of fathers winterized them, spending weekends adding cellars, coal furnaces, walls to separate rooms, a few feet to lengthen a living room. They installed bathtubs or showers, a stove, or an ice box. They all worked regular jobs as plumbers, carpenters, and pipefitters in downtown Manhattan. At five o'clock, they came home for supper and then put in another hour or two before bedtime on the bungalow-in-process. Saturdays and Sundays were spent on the construction projects, except for the Catholics who obeyed the "Remember to keep holy the Lord's day" commandment. While the dads worked, the moms watched the kids. Everybody helped everyone.

Our house was one of the largest on the block, with five small rooms—a kitchen, living room, two bedrooms (one for the boys and one for Catherine and me), and a dining room, which was originally supposed to be my parents' bedroom, but per my mother's insistence, they slept in the living room. The kitchen was very small, and my mother wanted all six of us to fit around one table for meals—especially dinner. So, she cashed in her Christmas Club savings, emptied her "change jar," and bought a brand-new dining room table and six chairs—maple, I think. She always made sure the table was covered with a neatly ironed tablecloth. Starched white lace curtains hung from the windows throughout the house. Doilies, which she crocheted herself, decorated the couch, the living-room chairs, and the bureaus in the bedrooms. Dad appreciated how fussy she was about our house and the dinner table; they bought a Castro convertible sofa for the living room where the two of them slept.

Sometimes I think that my longing for isolation is rooted in my feeling like an outsider all my young life. I belonged nowhere. Most comfortable when I was alone, I dreamed of walking with a sheet over my head and body, so no one could see me.

I lived as if that were true. As if I didn't hear the taunting of my brother and the neighborhood boys. As if I were proud, happy, beautiful. As if I didn't feel. My only pleasure came in the awareness that I never gave the boys the satisfaction of seeing me fall apart when they teased me. As if I didn't care about them or my height.

One's center
must really be
home.

But my body had other things to say—ugly, hurtful things. As I entered puberty, in lieu of pimples that the normal kids got, huge styes erupted on my eyelids, and boils appeared on my toes and under my arms. I hated what I looked like—a monster from a scary movie, with big lumps protruding from a huge fat head. My face, which I typically liked (except for my puffy cheeks), was ugly. There was no way to hide or bandage styes. The kids in school were freaked out by them and stayed away. And I couldn't stay home. Mom said I had to go to school.

She tried to help by giving me sunglasses, cutting holes in my shoes to make room for my swollen toes, and finally buying me sandals. But the styes were still there where everyone could see and be sickened by them. Or laugh at the fat gauze tubes where my toes had been. Somehow, I soldiered on, but I trembled through it all, praying that the Lord would make me "normal."

"Make me stop growing. Make the boils go away. Please Lord, can't this be enough? I don't think I can live like this."

Some days, somehow, the boils were worse than being almost six feet tall at eleven. When I was alone, I could escape the boys teasing me about my ungainly height. Not so with the styes—every time I washed my face or combed my hair, the mirror screamed how hideous my face was. Shame seethed inside me.

"Please Lord, I promise I'll become a nun if you want me to. Just please make them stop."

But He didn't answer. The boys were still in the alley. The styes continued to fester. I kept growing—alone except for my two normal-sized girlfriends, Marie and Mary. I was huge next to them, but we never acknowledged the difference between us. We pretended we were the same. There is such sweetness in that memory.

Then, as if God finally heard me and decided that I'd suffered enough, the styes disappeared before I reached high school. And by the time I was seventeen, I suddenly stopped growing, at six feet, one inch. I wasn't a giant! Thank you, Lord!

MORPHING

1963–1970

IN TIME, HEIGHT BECAME SOMETHING TO BE PROUD OF AS MOM HAD insisted. From feeling ugly and disgusting during my early years, I came to understand that what had been horrible in kid circles could morph into beauty in the adult world. In a matter of a year or two, I went from having no boys interested in me (even having to get a blind date for both my high school and college proms) to having as many guys as I wanted. It was a transformation that reshaped not only how others saw me but, more importantly, how I saw myself—a profound gift. I was suddenly in charge. Desired. Attractive. Along with two college girlfriends, Bridget and Joan, I started going to Friday night adult dances down on 86th Street in Manhattan's Germantown, which was known for its church and club-sponsored social events for immigrant German and Scandinavian men and women anxious to meet Americans. It was there that joy exploded.

As the tall women's department didn't tend to stock stylish clothes, Mom took it upon herself to start making my clothes, worthy of my Friday nights out. And she was good at it. Our first step was to go to Macy's and pick out a pattern and fabric—a magenta, turquoise, or navy taffeta or, my favorites, white peau de soie, black velvet, or burgundy matelassé. Then shortly before Mom cut out the dress, I'd begin to redesign it.

"Let's make angel sleeves that swish as I walk. Or maybe we could change this ballet neck to a V. Or how about adding a toss of emerald silk as a shawl, extra taffeta to the navy tulip dress to emphasize my waist?"

It was endless—me designing and Mom altering. Amazingly, for a person who was depressed herself and often cranky (or worse), she never lost her cool or made me feel bad for doubling her work. She never insisted I be satisfied with the original pattern. Instead, she was my willing—even eager—partner, sharing her own ideas about highlighting a sleeve or adding a jacket to complete a look. We were in heaven. Two neophyte designers giving birth to our just-conceived creation. She surprised me once with a voluminous black velvet shawl to complete the white strapless peau de soie! It was perfect! I loved it. She loved it. I felt myself walking differently, gliding almost. And I was ready. My first adult dance!

The dance hall was decorated with green velvet (the color of Christmas and the giant oak that kept watch over our beach when I was a girl), floor to ceiling drapes, and countless chairs and small tables covered with pristine white cloths. At the center of each table were four or five yellow tea roses in thin glass vases. Gold sconces hung from the walls behind a stage graced with dark-haired, gorgeous men tuning violins, cellos, and a piano. I did my best to ignore the rush of butterflies that filled my belly and chest as I approached the table I shared with Bridget and Joan, somehow managing to walk straight. After a few steps, I glided, truly. And as I had hoped, lots of men asked me to dance—many were Scandinavian and comfortable around tall women. They eagerly told me how beautiful I was and how much they'd like to see me again. What lovely moments in my life! Such Heaven!

After that I started dating and grew more and more confident, more daring, until I could walk into a room, pick out the most handsome guy, and set about attracting him to me. Which never took long. Eye contact is a magical potion. I was filled with a self-love that I hadn't thought possible. I wasn't Joan anymore. I was reborn. Between boils, styes, and endless height, I'd never dreamed I would embrace my height as desirable or sexy.

Only once before this, in my youth, did I glimpse the future of womanhood. I was twelve years old and walked along Edgewater

Beach in my brand-new white bathing suit with a huge red poppy along the side and discovered men's eyes following me. In that sexist, all too binary time, I couldn't imagine more joy.

TWISTED, TILTED

1963–1995

*Doctors keep referring to my tallness
and gravity. My body's in such a rush
to reach the dirt.*

SADLY, THE NEXT BLOW DIRECTED AT MY BODY FOLLOWED CLOSELY in tow. Just out of college, my friend Marie, a nursing school student, was practicing her newest skills and asked if she could check my back for scoliosis. Her diagnosis: yes, I had a curvature of the spine. Though I always believed I walked perfectly straight, I was reminded of the many times my parents told me to stand straight when it appeared that I was listing to the side. No one had mentioned scoliosis before—not my parents or our family doctor. Nor had anyone ever performed this test. Diagnoses like this were foreign to me. I'd never even heard of scoliosis, so I wasn't disturbed. Neither, it seemed, were my parents since they only ever casually reminded me to walk upright. Looking back, this was the first example of my parents' and my own denial of how my body needed to be cautiously watched and cared for.

BY THE TIME I WAS THIRTY, I DEVELOPED BACK PAIN AND WAS HOSPITALized in traction twice. I spoke to an orthopedist who confirmed that I indeed had scoliosis and "would someday need a fusion." My head exploded at the sound of the word, and a rush of fear filled my belly. I excused myself, left the office, and told no one of my official diagnosis. I resolved that I would never have spinal surgery. No surgeon would ever take a knife to my back. It was my first loving response to a body I had so hated growing up. I would protect my back. I just had to figure out how to minimize the pain. This wasn't hard at first—I just stopped lugging my heavy vacuum around the apartment and made do with a broom. I avoided any physical activity that would precipitate an attack.

But the pain soon accelerated from intermittent, to moderate, to constant and debilitating. I could not continue to ignore it. Yet, I waited until my early forties, when Alan, my handsome, loving, six-foot five-inch husband, crowned with a mass of chestnut curls that rivaled our son David's, urged me to confront the problem.

Sometimes he is Christ
reassuring me that I am loved,
but unlike Christ, who favors the soul,
my husband concentrates on the body
& what the body carries.

I had no choice. I was crushed and took this turn of events as my personal failure—a tendency that has plagued me all my life. Several months later I finally acquiesced. Thus began a series of appointments with the five top scoliosis specialists in New York City, which ended with unanimous agreement: fusion was the only option. Without it, I'd be in a wheelchair in a matter of years.

Since it's all we can know, he says,
it's the only thing we can count on.
It must then provide its own reward.

Dr. Engler was friendly, smart, and handsome. A talker. Chatty. Not what I expected from a top surgeon. In discussing major surgery with me, his vulnerable patient, he quickly moved away from my disability and the procedure itself and asked about my psychology practice. That led to him sharing that he was recently separated and on his way to divorce. When he discovered that David was a violinist, he rattled on about music. He proudly pointed to photos on the wall of young women and men doing high ski jumps post-surgery—people whose spines pre-surgery were as incapacitated as mine. Looking back, I recall my discomfort with his relaxed, confident manner. I wanted him to concentrate on the critical surgery he was about to perform, to focus on me and my back. He seemed to view my situation quite lightly. But that may have been his way of diffusing my anxiety, I reasoned.

He informed me that in addition to having a curved spine, mine was twisted. "You have a condition known as kyphosis," he announced.

He reassured me that he'd handled complicated cases like mine many times over, and I believed him. I was beginning to feel taken care of. He'd be the one to take me out of this cauldron of pain I was stewing in. I liked him, so did Alan, and he clearly liked us in return. Why shouldn't he be confident? He was an expert and had performed (assumably) hundreds of these fusions in his thirty years in practice. Alan too felt that Dr. Engler earned our confidence, and he was a down-to-earth nice guy instead of the stereotypical, standoffish surgeon. Then, on the morning of the surgery, he brought me a CD of Dvořák's Cello Suite to distract me from the pain. I was convinced. He was kind.

In the dark before surgery hands
dance over me hands smeared with blood
find quiet pockets hide things there
outside the sun cuts the ice on the Hudson
and I struggle like those ice fists
the current so hot rushing beneath—
Keep your hands off me!

The “first” surgery was actually two procedures, with one week between them. Collectively, the procedures required fusing several thoracic and lumbar vertebrae with titanium rods and screws, first through an incision in the belly, followed by one in my back a week later.

In some far-off city, two men send huge
cupped palms to grab my breasts broad
daylight no gasp or scream what most
astounds me is my silence the huge
breath sucked into my chest stuck there
gagging me leaving me voiceless the
merry-go-round not stopping

The results were mostly positive. Though the initial pain was excruciating, I came through the fusions almost pain-free! It was amazing. Dr. Engler proudly showed me the x-rays of my now-straightened spine. But when I asked to see the films showing the correction of the kyphosis, he said, “You didn’t have a kyphosis.”

Stunned and feeling lightheaded, I responded, “You told me I did. We discussed it pre-surgery.”

After that all is black. I have no memory of what he said or what transpired. One of the ways we defend ourselves psychologically against traumatic events is to repress them so that we have no recall of them. Following the surgery, I developed a condition called Flat Back, which means that the natural bend at the base of my spine is lost. I began to walk with a forward tilt, accommodating the twisted vertebrae. The only solution for me was to accept reality. I couldn’t believe that beyond the surgery itself, there was no pain! I kept waiting for it to erupt, but it didn’t. Months went by. Then years.

I’d heard of so many cases of people who had undergone fusion surgery that did little or nothing to control the pain. Mine was the opposite. My body was no longer my enemy. It twisted and tilted, yes. But the pain was gone.

Over there a huge rock like a great stone beast
ascends from the leaves: some great God of Life
whose time is now and who delivers herself
proudly out of the belly of the earth, her
wide mouth oozing green milk.

HOMES

2003

Regrettably, however, after several years of freedom, severe pain erupted with a vengeance. Just as I had in the years before the first fusion, I avoided standing at all costs. I became reclusive and depressed. Whenever vertical, I rushed to any chair, couch, or bed that would cushion and mute my screaming spine. The original surgeries hadn't gone far enough. The fusion needed to be extended into the sacral region.

For me, the spine is
home. I want to
leave my body,
soul slip out quietly,
float on its own for a while,
find some new home,
or perhaps become its own.

My new surgeon, Dr. O'Leary, was the county's leading scoliosis surgeon, but getting an appointment with him involved herculean patience. The only way to see him as a new patient was to have a referral from a neurologist who had previously ordered x-rays and an MRI or CT scan.

Dr. O'Leary was a big man, substantial, taller than me, with a bulky body like a guy who plays a mean game of Irish football. In fact, he was from Kerry, the same county in Ireland as my mother. But foremost, he was the man who called me early one evening over twenty years ago, never having met me. After reviewing x-rays of my first fusions and all my neurological tests, he asked how severe my pain was. I answered honestly. It was excruciating. "I imagine it is," he said. I started to cry, feeling so seen by that gentle question, followed by his rapid response, "I'll make some adjustments and we'll do the surgery on Thursday."

It's not the dark of night that frightens:
the dark that lies down gently on the trees
but never insists itself into my mind. Instead,
it's the dark at the end of the needle I fear,
that sends me where the mind no longer
is the mother I depend on. I no longer know
the shape of my own skin. The mind is my
only beacon, flashing red & green, the mother
who watches closely, follows every move,
sends me signals—when to wake, how to
bless, how to stop this knife from slipping.

And so, he performed the surgery that Thursday. Miraculously, once again, the pain slipped away. Since then, Dr. O'Leary has been the godfather of my spine. He has guided me through how to take care of it, and I do what he says. I am no longer alone. Amazingly, more than thirty years have passed, and I've been able to live my life—my new life—post-pain.

While I'm not cavalier about the mistake made by Dr. Engler and my tendency to walk with a bend in my gait, I would trade a tilt any day to be comfortable in my body again. Pain has a way of obliterating everything else—love, sex, joy. Its absence was and remains my miracle.

TALL FALLS

1990–2022

ALAS, SCOLIOSIS AND KYPHOSIS WEREN'T MY ONLY PHYSICAL CRISES. A few years after Dr. O'Leary's spinal surgery, while at the Thurnauer Music School, I found myself barely stifling an outburst at nine-year-old David for his inattention during that day's violin lesson. As I headed down the stairs from the music room to the lobby, David behind me, I tripped and tumbled—"F***!"— into the lobby swarming with parents and children walking with cellos, flutes, and violins. That accident resulted in a tri-malleolar fracture of my left ankle and a fusion surgery that kept me captive on the couch for months with numbing in my left ankle that continues to this day. Luckily, the fusion obliterated the pain, and after four months of physical therapy I was once again joyful and able to join my family in all their fun activities around East Hampton. Yet, even amid my renewed joy, I became very sober about my body's vulnerability.

In retrospect, I wonder what my life would have been if instead of accepting the physical injuries and flaws as a way of life, I had seen them as limitations. Would I be better prepared for aging? Would my slowing down bother me as much as it does? Though I love my quiet life and solitude, I hate my limitations. They infuriate me and rush me back to my years as an awkward teenager. Tall. Fall. Just one letter separates them. My family wouldn't have let me give in. Nor would my doctors. They insisted I'd be able to do everything I did before the pain took over. And more.

I imagine a body pale and capable.
In the pocket of my jacket, the pills
I forgot to take at breakfast: a splash
of blue, purple, red for hot flashes,
calcium, huge, white, and maternal,
the pale gold mirror of Vitamin E
keeping the skin from dying,
then the deep brandy Megavite
for everything else I'm missing.

GREEDY

Ongoing

WHILE MY CHECKERED PHYSICAL HISTORY SHAPED MY AGING AND deprived me of a sense of confidence in my body's strength, I resisted slowing down. It's true, I'm driven. I wish it were not the case, but all my life, I've been greedy to reach the next step, place, career. That's right, greedy. In fact, a friend who read this book in its early stages wondered why I described my behavior as greedy—a negative term.

"Why not courageous?" she suggested.

To answer that question, I look back to my childhood training in Catholicism, which regarded big appetites as excessive and sinful. Somehow describing myself as greedy diffuses the shamefulness that the Church would accuse me of and almost flaunts the behavior as acceptable in my eyes.

As a teenager, I was voracious in my wish to see what lay beyond our little hamlet in the northeast Bronx, so I went to college, became a teacher, and bought a gleaming red Buick Skylark (sadly, not a convertible, but Dad pleaded for my safety, so I complied). That beauty took me driving into the country every chance I got. I wanted to see everything. Each picturesque landscape and turn in the road. My challenge was to drive in a different direction each time I went out exploring, until I could see no more signs of civilization. No telephone wires. Definitely no people. I was happiest alone. I craved the beyond, the edge—Alaska, Antarctica, the vast Pacific—all "big nature." Away, surrounded by God and His breathtaking peaks, I felt normal-sized.

Even small. Huge landscapes gave me a sense of proportion that only a woman once referred to as Beanstalk can really appreciate.

I became greedy for certificates of status and accomplishments—magic carpets that would take me further from the ridiculing boys I grew up with and the expectations imposed on girls raised in tiny towns at the edge of the world. Hence, at fifteen, I wanted to be an architect, but that was out of reach for girls in the 1950s (at least the girls I knew), which led to a certificate in interior design in my early thirties. I've had multiple careers: teaching English to inner-city high school kids and later to privileged suburbanites; working as a guidance counselor for middle and high schoolers; college professing at St. John's University; and of course, treating adolescents and then adults (mostly women) for thirty years in my psychotherapy practice. I was already past forty when I began writing poetry. I earned a handful of degrees—bachelors, master's, PhD, and a second master's in creative writing. I've worked hard and enjoy working hard.

My appetites for learning and pleasure were and still are huge. If I want something, be it career or degree or the latest fashion, I go after it—steadfast and convinced that I could learn to do just about anything. But even now, with a life chock-full of accomplishments, I can't walk the streets of the neighborhood I grew up in without feeling oversized and threatened by the thought of teenaged boys lurking in the alleys and laughing at me.

LAZY

1980–Present

IRONICALLY, AS AMBITIOUS AS I AM, I'M ALSO LAZY. A SECRET SLOUCH, known only to Alan, David, and me. It was the product that was crucial, not so much the process. If I could skip a step on the road to success, I did. But I never cheated. I was too good a Catholic, and what would be the point? Where was the victory knowing that the "get" wasn't mine?

For me, everything was last minute—homework, all-nighters fueled by NoDoz pills and coffee during college and graduate school, even relying on tutors to drag me through graduate statistics. Sometimes, I'd skip looking up words I didn't understand (a habit that still embarrasses me!) and assume I'd figure them out from context, too impatient to stop. I hated studying and homework, cramming weeks of work into a night or two before a test. I preferred reading or watching TV. Still, I wanted to learn and understand the world, and school seemed like the place where that should happen.

There were only two things that ever leveled me, that I believed I couldn't accomplish. They erupted well into my late thirties, early forties. The first was becoming a mother—I never craved it as most women in my generation seemed to. I was convinced I wouldn't be good enough or that I'd resent the child for intruding on my life. I needed all my time to pursue the many goals I set for myself. Motherhood had been my mother's entire world—cooking, baking, laundry, food shopping, keeping track of four kids born over six years. I knew I didn't want that. Full-time and final, it would hold me back from the life I envisioned.

Once a woman was pregnant, her future was fixed. She'd be a mother for the rest of her life. I grew up Catholic during a time when abortion was illegal throughout the United States. In all areas of my life, I counted on the freedom of choice—having the ability to change directions if I had the mind to. But that wasn't possible after giving birth. The issue changed for me when I met and married Alan, my second husband—a man who very much wanted a child and was clearly invested in sharing childcare.

We gave birth to a splendid baby boy on a splendid July day in 1980. From the moment I set eyes on him, I was in love. We named him David. There was room for the three of us—David, Alan, and me.

The night our son was born, there were no
taxis & it was too far to walk. But he found
a wheelchair & gently helped me in.
& as if
time spun itself as far back as he insisted,
traffic, obeying him, settled down &
moved over, perhaps even recalling its
own holy history as donkeys & cattle,
the street a dirt path.
Make way,
his silence commanded. There were
no screeching horns, just vehicles
prayerfully slowing then stopping
as will happen in the path of any
sacred rite. I am frightened. "I am
with you." I'm not ready. I won't
make it. "He's our baby." I can't
do it. Oh God! He is coming I
can't do this "We will do it."
Thy Will be done.

The second thing that I believed I would never accomplish was becoming a poet. Dilettante that I was, I assumed you couldn't learn to write. I believed it was a gift that sprung fully formed from anyone with talent, the mysterious element required for creating any fine art. That it was God-given, and it depended on whether He decided to give it to you. To complicate things further, I believed that He gave a particular talent to only one person in a family, and He'd already made my brother Sonny a very talented artist. If everyone was blessed with one talent, and I got very good grades in school and was considered smart, maybe that was my gift. In any case, except for two prose recountings of lost love, I completely avoided writing until my early forties.

Poetry was the peak of Mount Everest when it came to natural, God-given gifts. Eventually, when I decided to try, my efforts felt flimsy. From time to time, I'd pour myself a glass of wine in the evening while Alan played tennis, and I'd sit down to try to write a poem. But by morning's light, the truth was undeniable—what I'd written was trite and uninspired. It became painfully clear that I didn't have talent. I was devastated.

That awareness led to my first clinical depression. I contacted a psychiatrist who I referred patients to for medication consultation, and we agreed that I would start therapy, try an antidepressant medication, and, with a friend's help, enroll in a beginners' poetry writing workshop. If there was such a thing as beginners' workshops, maybe there was something I could learn about writing poems, even without natural talent. I quivered each time it was my turn to read a draft aloud, but I was relentless. I devoted as many hours to writing as necessary, and because I was so critical of everything I wrote, the rest of life—including my family and friends—was pushed to the sidelines, squeezed into an hour or two.

My journey through discovering myself as a poet continues today, but regrettably as time moved on, I'm only writing when I have something to say or when a poem calls to me, i.e., *I'm lazy!* The concept of sitting with an empty page until it is covered with new lines and stanzas is unappealing. I can't tolerate waiting for inspiration to strike. If I sit down with the intention to write but no inspirational spark behind it, I'll end up window-shopping online. Not mind-expanding or challenging. But fun. And I never tire of looking at beautiful clothes.

LOVE AFFAIR

1953

LONG BEFORE SHE BECAME MY SEAMSTRESS, MOM AND I SHOPPED for my clothes. It was a favorite pastime for many mothers and daughters during the 1950s and '60s and certainly was for us. It was the beginning of my lifelong romance with fashion. Because Mom insisted my height was something to be proud of, she dressed me in women's clothes from the time I was twelve. Dad would drive us to the subway at Westchester Square in "Gorgeous George," our spiffy bright blue Chevy sedan that had thankfully replaced "Leapin' Lena," our ancient jalopy that embarrassed all of us Cusack kids. Off Mom and I would go, first to Bloomingdale's at 59th Street, then to Macy's at 34th. We spent many Thursday nights and Saturday afternoons shopping the racks.

When the traffic on the floor thinned out, the sales ladies would get involved, offering opinions, and we'd have a fashion show. As I tried on coats, skirts, and dresses, I twisted and swirled for them just as Loretta Young did on her TV show. I fell in love with how I looked. I adored the brightness that lit Mom's eyes and her smile as she admired me in each new outfit.

Her familiar darkness gave way to pride. "Oh, Joanie, you look so beautiful! Nobody wears clothes like you."

With my mother and the sales ladies in a circle around me, I believed I was beautiful. Mom was unrelenting, searching out new styles till the store lights started to flicker. I never knew how she paid for the clothes, but she'd quiet my anxiety saying, "What do you think I have my charge cards for?"

Those days calmed my view of myself as awkward, clumsy, oversized. Since my mother passed away, it's no surprise that my love affair with clothes continues. It was a comfortable and easy switch to peruse fashions online as I relax in my pink cuddly bathrobe rather than visit the real-life department stores that I no longer have the energy, strength, or time for. Besides, clothes shopping is just not the same without her. Those many years ago, she was her softer, gentler self. Sadly, though, I never saw her respond so tenderly to my siblings. Looking back, I think she felt that given my height and the boys torturing me, I needed her more. Approaching eighty, it's such a pleasure bringing her back through writing.

As I step back now, several things occur to me. The first is that I describe myself and my mother as unrelenting, and it's apt. Memory teaches me that our pace and intention were the same—fierce and directed. I wish she were here so I could thank her, even shower her with lilies of the valley, her favorite. In writing this I realize it was she who saved me emotionally when I was a girl. She insisted that my height was beautiful, and I was beautiful. Not a monster. Buying me clothes that fit and complemented my features kept me alive, strong, fighting. She refused to let me drown in the boys' taunting and the despair they caused. Reflecting on this now fills me with an unexpected sense of joy.

Following a career in psychotherapy, the analytical part of my brain can't help but interject. I refer to her as "Therapist Joan" and she joins in my inner monologue on a regular basis. As is the case when she comments:

> In aging we have the capacity to resurrect emotions, events, people—study them, turn them around. It's the mental reverse of falling.

Physically, with age, my body keeps falling, but in my mind and imagination, I am rising still.

FRACTURED

2020

Another sleepless dawn, walking in the woods
listening for God. At my feet there's a green
parade of small things, a rusted silver oil can,
the white of startled birch, a few daffodils
out where the earth dips down.

BORN DURING A TIME WHEN MOST WOMEN DIDN'T EXERCISE, IT was natural for me to ignore my body. In the fifties, boys and men wanted muscles; girls and women with muscle were seen as too masculine unless they excelled at a sport—a rarity for women compared to men. Add to that the fact that I was raised staunch Catholic, a religion that regarded the body as the temple of sin. There was little acknowledgment of the body as a source of health and vitality, as what allowed us to walk, dance, sing, or swim. No classes in Catholic school celebrated the riches of the body, its strengths and vulnerabilities. Instead, school and church taught that the body should be guarded against sin—sexual thoughts, desires, and, above all, sexual acts. The rules were strict. The very thought of a sin was a sin.

But I was safe. I had no sexual thoughts or desires.

Therapist Joan says:

`Or you had repressed them.`

Save for a passion for clothes, in my youth, I ignored my body. It could take care of itself. It could keep pace.

That said, it's been a relief to be relatively free of those painful adolescent feelings when all I knew of my body was its relentless height and the fear that I would never stop growing. What remains is a lasting impatience with my body—likely rooted in those childhood traumas, compounded by injuries, major surgeries in adulthood, and the inevitable process of aging. The challenge as I approach eighty is that I still don't like to listen to my body. It's already stolen too much of my time.

Lately it cries out, "Be careful! Slow down!"

Yet I still walk barefoot on well-polished floors, wearing maxi dresses that drape down to my toes. I wrap myself in a seven-foot shawl and lug an overstuffed tote in one hand and a mug of coffee in the other. Then, a few weeks ago, in the 3 a.m. pitch dark, I slipped on a wet spot in the living room, injuring my foot and sacrum. It was my third fall in a year. At first, Alan and I tried to downplay the injury, both insisting there was no need to call David or an ambulance. We were sure I didn't need a hospital, so I remained on the floor, wrapped in blankets until we could call a doorman who would help me back into bed. Alan, strong as he is (in body and mind) couldn't do it alone.

But when morning finally came, the doorman told us that it was against building policy for him to assist me physically.

"You'll have to call 911," he said.

I dreaded the thought of being wheeled on a stretcher through the crowded lobby, an older woman flanked by two laughably young officers. But eventually, we made the call, and I was taken to the hospital. X-rays confirmed fractures in both my foot and sacrum. My head spun and the burning reignited in my belly. As soon as I was able to return home and hobble in my boot and walker, I scheduled an appointment with Dr. O'Leary.

I trembled as I sat in his exam room. Had the fall dislodged the neighboring vertebrae? Had I injured my already very vulnerable back? He assured me that although the sacrum was in fact fractured, it would heal on its own. Amazingly, the fusion was intact. Relieved beyond measure, I was elated by the news, yet unforgiving with myself. As soon as I left the office, I taunted my image reflected in the elevator door—my clumsy awkward self, hobbling with the hideous boot and walker.

When I got home, David called to ask about the appointment and said he was coming over with his girls, my beautiful granddaughters, to cheer me up. That they did. I could feel the depressive cloud lifting as I always did in their presence. Shortly after they arrived, five-year-old Cassidy suggested a "china party," a tea party featuring my antique blue and white china dishes. Elodie, two, was soon napping on the couch, so it was safe. Turning the key, Cassidy gingerly opened the hand-painted cabinet that had belonged to Alan's mom. We removed the teapot, sugar bowl, creamer, and the small matching plates for our cookies. I brought silver spoons and found a lace cloth for our table. Apple juice was substituted for tea, and we sat together chatting about our favorite memories—Friday sleepovers, reading together, visiting the carousel under the Brooklyn Bridge, our favorite place, and of course sipping "tea"—with pinkies aloft, she reminded me—in very queenly fashion. We delicately munched our chocolate chip cookies, and the afternoon passed with no thought of my visit to Dr. O'Leary. Oh, the glory of it! In the company of these two lovely grandgirls, depression seemed to disappear and joy reigned.

A KINDNESS

2020

But tea parties don't last forever. I woke in the middle of the night to my heart banging in my chest. I'm old.

My body felt tired. I avoided going out, anticipating my exhaustion after any activity. All I wanted to do was rest. A red flag waved—this was undoubtedly depression, coupled with my struggle to gracefully accept the signs of aging. I used to welcome illness, a cold or sinus infection, as relief, an excuse to rest. It gave me a legitimate reason to cancel appointments, skip visits with friends, or take a break from work.

For years, I loved smoking pot because of the creative energy it gave me. I could write, rearrange the bedroom, hang pictures, tackle an overstuffed closet. It returned me to my original pace—fast, faster. It kept the feeling of aging at bay, though it was far from a sustainable approach. Eventually, I stopped smoking because it was too closely tied to smoking cigarettes—a habit I'd quit once and couldn't risk relapsing into. David was sympathetic, so he bought me a cannabis vape, but that triggered chest congestion.

So, I've given up pot both as a treat and energizer. Packages remain unopened. Chores go unattended.

Is it laziness as I've often believed? Or is it the fact that I now prefer a slower life? I need a slow pace to write, to open my memories and imagination, to process almost eight decades of rapid living. Reflection is far more interesting than doing chores or opening packages.

I've often wondered if my falls are an indication of my unconscious need to slow down and my inability to give myself permission to do so.

I can't. Now that I'm physically restricted and the years continue to take their toll, I imagine my unconscious is relieved—I don't have to rush. I can rest even when I'm not sick. My body offers permission for the slow life—in fact, insists on it.

FANTASY

2018 / Ongoing

"I'M AT WAR WITH MY BODY."

I wrote that in a poem many years ago, and David brings up the line often, even though the time and sentiment of the observation are long gone. At forty-three, with his abundant chestnut curls and a smile that would melt glaciers, he has developed into a man with a superego of mega proportion whose task it is to cure me of my tendency to disrespect my body. He's convinced that I need constant surveillance and reminds me every time I do something that proves he's right. A prime example: the winter night he picked me up at the airport and caught me without hat, scarf, or gloves wearing only a thin jacket.

"You gotta start taking care of yourself," he angrily snapped.

David and I talk often and intently. He worries about my disregard for my vulnerability and my cavalier attitude toward my body. I know he's right.

Everyone tells me how young I look, and it's true. I still color my hair red with blonde highlights and wear it long. I seem to believe that I'm immune from aging. But I'm not. Bruises take much longer to heal; my skin is dry and crinkling and cries out from neglect. I have arthritis in my knees and back, osteoporosis in my hips, and osteopenia in my spine.

The illusion of freedom is the fantasy of invulnerability. Nothing's going to happen to me. All that counts is that I'm doing what I choose. It has to do with design, I rationalize. Grace. I know fashion, what works and what doesn't. To avoid tripping, I could wear shorter dresses to break the flow and pants that cut off at the ankle. The collision of my eye for art and the needs of my aging body reminds me of Cassidy insisting that, despite the freezing temperatures, she doesn't need a coat! She doesn't want to cover her new Elsa dress. Suddenly, I'm looking at my small self and my adult self. My granddaughter and I are kindred spirits when it comes to clothes. I love it!

Very wise and always confident, David is vocal about his anger with me. Over the years, his frustration has crystallized. It's been his way to avoid disappointing me. Always a sensitive son, he never wants to hurt my feelings. But these days he has no problem expressing his aggravation.

"You don't know how many times you've said this before and nothing happens—you start walking, but sooner or later you stop. You always stop!" he would say, exasperated. "You should be walking 30 minutes every day." Oh Dear Lord, my beloved heart-speak is giving up on me!

"Every day for the rest of your life!" Then softening his tone, he tells me to do less if I'm not up to a full half hour. Before I could chime in that I had started walking again, he continues, "And forget fashion! Dresses, skirts, pants above the ankle! Or you'll fall. You already have! And where's your hat? It's freezing out!"

I can hear myself railing at my sister Catherine ten years ago: "If you won't do it for yourself, do it for your son!" I recall waking one day a few decades ago thinking, Oh my God! I don't want David to remember me as always sick. It finally occurred to me that he had no choice.

When he was a boy, crises befell me on a regular basis. Before and after my surgeries, Martha, our nanny, took him to violin lessons and supervised his practice sessions, and Alan taxied him to and from school and took care of him in the preschool morning and evening rituals. They loved cooking together—apple pancakes, hot dogs, and their specialty, bacon, tomato, and onion sandwiches. They were a team in the kitchen. I was grateful, of course, as well as guilty. And sad. What was missing from David's young life was the company of a mom who was readily available to focus on him and his interests. Instead, he had to place me first in his life and protect me from any danger or disappointment. Our positions were reversed. I was the child and he the caregiver. He insisted that he was fine, and he and his dad were helping each other. But I knew he was lonely and anxious and didn't ask for anything. He could take care of himself, he insisted. Sadly, he had to.

I remember a day when he was around five. Alan and I were in the midst of a marital struggle. This wasn't our first, and because we were both raw and David was vulnerable, he heard a lot of what transpired between us. Alan tried to reassure him, but he was also honest, preparing David for the possibility of our separation.

I was resting in bed when he came slowly, quietly into the room asking, "Mom, Dad told me about you and him and how he may not be living with us anymore. Are you okay?"

I, too, had to be honest with him. I told David I was sad, but that Dad was right when he said we might separate, and I didn't know what was going to happen. I told him that we were trying to work things out but if we did separate, he should know that we both loved him, and our relationship with him would not change. I also told him that we understood how sad he was, and we'd do all we could to protect him and our marriage. But sometimes the only answer is to separate—in fact sometimes it helps that both people have a chance to think more deeply about the marriage and decide if it can be saved. David was pensive but accepted what I had to say.

We hugged and he said, "I love you, Mom. I think I'll go back to my homework."

My heart ached for all three of us, and that heartache has stayed with me, always just beneath the surface. I wished with all my heart that we had a second child so that David would have someone to share and process this potential rift in our family. But alas, David was alone.

Alan did move out for a short period, but neither of us could bear separating. We loved each other too much to sacrifice our lives together. We started marital therapy. Our marriage healed and grew from the careful work we did and has remained so. Sometime later I wrote this poem—a tribute to David, Alan, and me.

So many people wake inside these marriage walls:
parents, God, nuns. But the child is holiest.
Advocate for each side. & they listen, trusting
the way his mind makes sense of their world:
sifting it, turning it, then returning it clarified.
Like Scribes in the Temple surrounding that
first Holy Child, they listen as he teaches them,
"Mom! Let it go. Back off!" The husband
gratefully echoed. Then "Dad!
Say something! Don't just criticize."
And she hears someone in back of
the curtain repeating her lines.

One of the ways I escape from the sadness that accompanies these memories is to recognize the joyful ones, too. And there were plenty. I recall the summer when David was eight, and he attended violin camp at Ithaca College. We stayed at the elegant but relaxed Pig Snout Hotel (David's self-proclaimed name for it), with an oversized color TV, VCR, and vending machines full of his favorites, Kit Kats and Skittles (sugar-conscious mom was on vacation). We watched *Police Academy* and *Planes, Trains & Automobiles,* and ate dinners at Pastabilities—spaghetti and meatballs for him, linguine with clam sauce for me. After the final performance, where he played Bach's Minuet No. 1 along with a chorus of violins and cellos, David and I, flushed with pride, drove home to East Hampton, our Happy Place.

It was common for psychotherapists to take a month-long vacation period, so all through the month of August, it was just the two of us with Alan visiting from New Jersey on weekends. David and I squeezed as much fun as we could into each day: swimming, more swimming, movies, and a half hour of practice. We finished the days off with Vivaldi's Violin Concerto blaring as David flew from the house, down the back steps, and into the pool. We took long drives to Montauk for more pasta dinners in one of our favorite restaurants, talking, laughing, talking, laughing—so thrilled to have this private time for the two of us. Oh, Glory! For me, there are no greater mom moments than these!

But despite a life that abounded with fun, David has spent most of his days worrying about me. Particularly about me falling. This saddens me, but it's true. He lived through my hysterectomy when he was ten years old, my broken ankles (the first when I was pregnant with him), ankle fusion, and two spinal fusions. He has never known me to be physically strong. Last year, I caught pneumonia twice!

He doesn't take his eyes off me. "Careful, Mom. Watch that step—it's chipped."

He knew nothing of the freedom a child feels growing up with a parent's strength, assurance, and protection. The freedom to not see the world as imminently dangerous.

These are the reflections I focus on in the midst of COVID quarantine, while Alan and I are confined to our Brooklyn apartment—as the ambulances shriek by on their way to Beth Israel Hospital, as the news reports thousands of people who have died each day, and as we listen to stories of nurses and doctors exhausted, blind with hard work. Yet they prevail. At 7 each night, we remind them how much we value their herculean efforts with the rattling and banging of pots and pans coming from windows of skyscrapers and apartment buildings around us—our tribute to the angels who watch over us. Our heroes and saviors, restoring hope, if only for a moment, the only hope left.

II

Heartsick

THE HEART THING

2019

Another October
measures
what is finished.

NOT ONLY AM I GRAPPLING WITH MY OWN AGING, BUT MY OLDER sister, Catherine, is showing signs of physical challenges as well. She's eighty-two and has her own litany of physical problems. Like most aging people, she talks about them a lot. And I don't like it. As a therapist, I'm aware of how indelible sibling relationships are, but at the same time, I know that people change as they grow older. Negotiating those changes is a challenge. In our case, the four-year age difference precluded closeness when we were kids, yet Catherine has become increasingly dependent on me as we age. That frightens me, not only because of the burden it places on me, but because it highlights another pitfall of our dependency on others for care. It reminds me of my pre-fusion helplessness. I shudder at the thought of it.

In any case, three weeks before the onset of the COVID pandemic, Catherine was sick, and Alan and I made our way to Mt. Sinai Hospital to visit her and speak with her doctors. I hate hospitals. On the drive, I obsessed over what I disliked most about them—I settled on the relentless stench that invades everything and everyone and has me convinced that I'll never wash it off my clothes or out of my nose. That putrid smell of things gone wrong, bodies failing, and twice overcooked food. The very thought of hospitals and hospital food makes me gag. Having spent many days, even months, in hospitals taking care of my mother when she had her cancer, my father with his fractured hip, and Catherine with her multiple surgeries, I was pissed at her for getting herself admitted again. If she had paid more attention to her own care, it wouldn't be dropped in my lap all the time, I seethed. It occurs to me that I sound like David complaining about me.

But, miracle of miracles, when we passed through the hospital door, there was no odor. We might just as easily have been walking into a store or library. The lobby was bright and cheerful with its huge vases of magenta bougainvillea. Relieved, I handed over my license to the pretty girl with the perfectly plaited braids that reached her tush, who was checking IDs at the desk. She couldn't have been more than twenty.

My belly tightened again at the thought of seeing Catherine, who was once vigorous and healthy just like this receptionist, now weak and infirm. Instead, as I headed toward her hospital room, I heard her laughing and joking with someone—maybe her roommate or one of the nurses. I immediately relaxed. She'd found her cronies. She might as well have been out on her stoop in Edgewater, joking with her girlfriends. She'd be okay here. I'd be okay here, too.

"Hi, Honey," she greeted me, smiling. "Thanks for coming." Noticing Alan behind me, she was visibly thrilled. "And you brought my angel! Hi Alan!" She then returned to me without missing a beat, "Where'd you get that hat? I love it!" She pointed to the matching navy beanies Alan bought us. I took mine off and plopped it on her head.

"You look cute," I laughed, kissing her cheek. And she was cute. Remarkably, she was happy, pale and sick as she was. My resentment over her illness dissolved. I couldn't stay angry with her for very long.

THE FALLING

2019

Leaves ripen,
let go.
The sun moves on.

SEVENTY-PLUS YEARS A SMOKER AND THE OLDEST OF THE FOUR OF us, Catherine has always insisted that no one tell her what to do. She isn't quitting. She says she knows what her body can handle—she's evaded a cancer scare, had emphysema, overcome an abdominal aneurysm (repaired surgically three times), and had a diseased kidney removed. But now her heart is functioning well below normal. She's scared. We all are.

"I was always convinced I'd be the last of us to go. Figured I was made of iron stock like Dad," she once told me. I used to believe that too.

While she's in Mt. Sinai Hospital confined to bed, she can't smoke. The doctor gave her a nicotine patch to ease the cravings, and though she isn't complaining to me, she expresses her frustration to Michael, her son. In any case, if this next surgery is successful, and the team manages to open the ventricles with a stint and restore her heart's function, I'm convinced she'll be back to the cigarettes, smug that she dodged a bullet again, as she knew she would. She speaks to the Lord and His Blessed Mother every night.

"They won't let anything bad happen to me," she peacocks.

The heart thing, as she refers to it, is a shock to all of us. She has shown no signs of heart problems aside from brief episodes of high or low blood pressure around her surgeries. That is, if you don't count an abdominal aneurysm as a heart problem. But that was the one condition she carefully monitored with her surgeon, undergoing quarterly testing to ensure her numbers stayed within a safe range. Low numbers meant that the most recent repair was holding; high numbers meant another surgery was needed. According to her medical team, the aneurysm was under control when she was admitted to the hospital. But then she fell when trying to get out of bed.

It was the falling that sent her to the hospital in the first place. She had become even more difficult to reach by phone, and Michael had returned to his family in upstate New York for Christmas. Catherine told me she'd try to come to East Hampton to be with Alan, David and his family, and me for the holidays. She planned to get a car to drive her to the Jitney as she usually did, and we'd pick her up on the other side. But in the end, she was too tired to go anywhere.

I wasn't surprised and even a bit relieved—I'd have my family to myself and wouldn't need to take care of her. I have always preferred to keep gatherings small and intimate, especially visits over several days. Catherine would have been fine, but my mood would have been heavier and less festive, as it usually was with Catherine there.

None of the Handlers felt lighthearted as the holidays started; we had some repair work to do to regain a sense of normalcy. I was still hobbling along in a boot, and David was furious with me for causing my third fall. Best to endure the holiday without the added company. Catherine insisted she was fine staying home. She had plenty of Meals on Wheels food in the freezer but was simply wiped out. As I think back, she sounded more tired than usual.

"I'll be okay," she'd said. I vaguely remember calling her on Christmas. I hope I did. I'm so bad with the phone.

The following week, Alan, David, his two girls, and I went on a Handler family vacation to Mexico. When we arrived home, Michael texted me that Catherine had left several days' worth of dishes unwashed (very unlike her) and was sleeping more than usual. Then he found her two days in a row on the floor—she had fallen and had tried to get up but couldn't. We both knew it was time to call 911.

When the EMS team arrived, Catherine refused to go with them. She took pride in being the eldest and most in control, and she wouldn't be persuaded. No meant no.

"My Blessed Mother won't let anything bad happen to me. I speak to her every night," she insisted.

But where was your Blessed Mother when you fell two other times that week? I sneered silently.

I finally called on Alan to speak with her—he was the only one she'd listen to. The next time we called 911, she agreed to go with them. Her heart rate was just 15 percent of capacity when she was admitted. She was profoundly sick.

In the hours that followed, I found myself thinking about Catherine's devotion throughout her life. Growing up, she and I attended 6 a.m. Mass with Dad during Lent and Advent, but she never seemed as paranoid about sin as I was. As a young teenager, she broke several of Mom's rules—smoking and hanging out at her friend's house after school—nothing serious in retrospect but major offenses in Mom's eyes. Generally speaking, Catherine was a normal teenaged girl. As an adult, at some point she stopped going to Sunday Mass, but she maintained her commitment to and trust in the Lord and His Blessed Mother for her whole life. Despite her distance from the formal Church and its rules, she retained great faith. She believed that she was loved and cared for by her heavenly family. I hope that minimized her loneliness.

PINK CHEEKS, SOFT SILVER HAIR

2020

Something
in the sound of it
fists pounding

MY ANXIETY IS CONSTANT AND I'M FALLING DEEPER INTO depression. I hate seeing Catherine's shrunken body and spindly arms—though her pink cheeks and soft silver hair, cropped as always, still offer glimpses of her old self. The medical team offers conflicting reports: another change of plans, another infection.

Thankfully, Alan comes with me to the hospital. He knows I'm floundering after weeks of confronting her fragile body and condition. It frightens me to see how sick she is, how painfully thin she's become. Yet her gratitude is palpable. She lights up when she sees us, her happiness somehow unwavering. How is she managing to hold on?

Between Michael, Alan, David, my nieces, Maureen and Dolores (Sonny's daughters), and me, we do our best to keep her company on weekends. Meanwhile, Michael returns home to care for his wife, who is facing her own health challenges, including an upcoming knee replacement surgery.

Michael is my hero—tough and unfaltering. He's in charge and handles that responsibility with grace. He works at his teaching job every day and comes directly to the hospital afterward. Somehow, he nobly tends to his mother, as well as his wife, his stepmother, and mother-in-law, all of whom are seriously ill. His stamina amazes all of us—how closely he monitors his mother and her care. Their devotion to each other mixes with their sassy banter, which keeps all of us laughing.

Years before, Michael was in a horrific accident that paralyzed him and kept him bedridden for months. His wife was not strong enough to care for him by herself, and Catherine insisted that he stay in her home, where she nursed him 24/7 for months.

"He's my son," she had announced proudly.

Looking at him today, no one would surmise that he'd been so severely injured years before. Once paralyzed, he doesn't even have the hint of a limp now.

Two procedures are under consideration for Catherine now—a stint and a pacemaker. First, the decision had been to go with the stint, but that needed to be cancelled. It was too risky. She's still far too weak. The medical team has now decided to continue with heavy doses of IV medications to encourage her heart rate to improve. They manage to get it up to 40 percent, and we're celebrating. She's nearly ready for the pacemaker, the charm that will bring her back to us. If her heart rate drops below a sustainable rate, the pacemaker will kick in and increase the pace. She's scheduled for the following day, but not before two major blood infections are discovered and she's treated with large doses of antibiotics. The surgery can't be performed until the infections are eliminated. This will take another fourteen days. The wait seems endless.

The infections finally disappear, and the team schedules the pacemaker again. After all the aborted surgeries, I'm not very hopeful that this one will be different. Alan and I arrive by 7 a.m. But when we step off the elevator, there is a commotion on the floor, particularly around Catherine's room. *Oh my God, she's dead!* I think, belly blasting and head spinning.

A nurse takes my arm and invites me to join Catherine. "There are no operating rooms available, and the team of surgeons and cardiologists are ready," she says. "They can't take the chance of delaying the surgery once again, so they will operate in her room."

"In her room? Isn't that dangerous?" I respond. But the nurse assures me that they do this from time to time when the surgical schedule is backed up. She explains that the space is being sanitized, and when it is, they'll perform the procedure. She suggests I keep Catherine company before it begins.

The room is a commotion of doctors of all sizes and genders in white surgical coats and masks giving instructions, ordering equipment. One surgeon promises to find us when they finish. He seems to understand how long we've been waiting, as does the chief cardiologist, who oversees this remarkable display of efficiency, good humor, and medical expertise.

"Hi, Honey. Can you believe it's finally happening?!" Catherine laughs, "I know I can't. And would you look at this room? All these nice doctors and nurses with their fancy machines are here to get my heart going! My lazy heart!"

I can't believe her spirit isn't diminished. Speechless, I make my way to her bedside, kiss her, and tell her we'll be waiting for her on the other side of propofol.

"Great! See you later, Honey!"

ON THE FIRST NIGHT OF ENFORCED QUARANTINE

2020

Soon
only oak leaves
will cling.

As I leave Catherine, I am trembling. Operated on in her own room! It's such a public event. The whole floor is buzzing, knowing that something unusual is taking place. Surely, there is a precedent for this, I assure myself as I head to the waiting area where the rest of the family is assembled, pausing to remind at least three people where they can find us when the surgery is over. And so, the family team keeps watch for the next hour and a half until our girl comes back to us.

"Well, here we are again, Family, another hospital, another surgery for Aunt Catherine," Maureen says, trying to cheer us up, spotlighting how quick we are to get together—especially for hospital visits and funerals, with an occasional wedding thrown in. To pass the time, we trade our favorite anecdotes about Catherine. For me, it's the bright spring day we met her in the rehab garden after her abdominal surgery. The tulips and lilies blushed their many shades of orange, pink, and coral. Catherine was gleeful, plopped in her wheelchair, and once outside, made a beeline for the table where several patients, men mostly, were smoking. Undaunted, she spun her chair toward two other smoking duos until she managed to get a cigarette. I couldn't believe it. But it was Catherine. Rather than yell, as is my way, I pretended I didn't see her. She was too sick to be shouted at.

Though the pacemaker is successfully inserted, she remains in the hospital for several more weeks. They can't control her blood pressure—it drops over fifty points simply when she stands up. What is happening? I'm more afraid than ever, starting to see signs that we might be losing her. Maybe the pacemaker isn't the solution. Not for her.

Not for me either. I also have low blood pressure that drops when I stand, but nowhere near this severe. Is this a hint of what's waiting for me? The thought terrifies me—that we share this fragile thread of vulnerability.

"The bathroom's right there. Why would I call the nurse? She's busy with all her other patients," Catherine snaps, once again in denial of how sick she's really been. She is finally accepted into a rehab facility close to her home and convenient for Michael. Hopefully, that will help her build her strength and bring her back to health. Michael tells the staff that she is a fall risk, but regrettably, she is left unattended and tries to get out of bed. Not surprisingly, she falls.

She is taken to yet another hospital where it is determined that the fall has caused a tear in the aneurysm repair, resulting in a slow leak. Lenox Hill Hospital admits her for observation, and while it is clear that the leak must be fixed, her surgeon decides it can wait two weeks until she is released from the hospital. Then we can take her to the specialist's office to assess the damage.

In the meantime, we start to look for a new rehab facility but delays arise due to a glitch with her insurance. Michael gets approval to have her return to a rehab center she's been in before, but I am adamant that we hold out. I wasn't happy with the level of care she'd received there during a previous incident. David spoke with a friend from a state assessment group that evaluated nursing homes; she confirmed the rehab center to be mediocre, at best.

It is the only time that Michael and I disagree. His focus is on expediting admission and mine is on holding out for a better institution.

He ultimately agrees to wait, and soon we get word that she is to be admitted to Schervier Rehabilitation Center, the highly recommended rehab we were hoping for. My father received wonderful care there. We are all relieved and thrilled.

That said, despite the pacemaker, after a series of missteps on the part of the medical community and the rehab center, following eleven endless weeks in the hospital, and on the night after the COVID-19 enforced quarantine was imposed, Michael calls me at 1:18 a.m.

"I just got a call from the rehab doctor. Mom passed away at 12:37."

I am stunned.

"Oh my God, NO! How could this happen? What about the pacemaker? Did she know she was dying? Was she in pain, was she alone?"

Michael has no answers. He too is in shock. I put the phone down in a stupor, a state that persists for weeks, months. There's no escaping the news: Catherine—big sister, Dad's Bobba, loving mother, Sonny's pal, best friend and confidante, bingo champ, career secretary, generous, funny, wisecracking, Blessed Mother's beloved daughter—is dead.

COMPLICIT

2012 / 2021

On the table,
three red roses.

IT IS APRIL 2021 AND NIGHT DEMONS ATTACK: *IT'S YOUR FAULT. YOU triggered her death by usurping control and insisting that we hold off for a better rehab. It cost her life! Why couldn't you have stayed out of it? Have followed Michael quietly. Let him lead without questioning his judgment.*

It's the one thing Michael and I haven't talked about. I'd hoped these thoughts would dissipate over time, but they gnaw at me still. Another obsession. Ready to pounce. Crisp, clear, accusing. I need to talk to Michael. To ask him to forgive me.

Ten years ago, I worried that I'd accelerated Dad's death by encouraging him to walk freely in my house in East Hampton—his favorite place to be besides his own small house with the worn brown leather chair he lived in all his adult life. He had his stick to balance him.

"You're safe, Dad," I assured him.

I was so proud of his age and resilience and couldn't bear to see him afraid. He'd never been vulnerable in my eyes. I needed him to be strong as he'd always been. But he wasn't safe. He fell early one morning on his way to the bathroom. I was sleeping in the room beside him for just such an emergency. I woke to his stick banging on the floor. Surgery was the only option if he was to avoid being stuck in a wheelchair for the rest of his days. His hip was fractured. He was ninety-nine and a half, and insisted that Alan, David, and I help him make the decision. What was the prognosis for a man of his age having surgery?

"He has the heart of a fifty-year-old," the ER doctor assured us.

We all concurred. Surgery was immediate and successful, but alas, he passed away two nights later from pneumonia, a common cause of death among the hospitalized elderly. Losing him broke my heart.

Now, Catherine.

Was I complicit in her death? She was finally admitted to our preferred rehab and later that night she had a heart attack. I keep repeating the same questions to myself, to Alan, to anyone who'll listen. What about the pacemaker? Where was the staff? Oh, dear God, did she suffer? Was it a heart attack or had she given up when she realized she was in yet another facility and would not be able to see her son because of the COVID-19 quarantine? Was she just too tired to handle another battle?

The shock of her death was mixed with the unimaginable horror of the pandemic. Mandatory quarantine was imposed the same day that Catherine was admitted to the rehab. Michael was not allowed into the facility with her to set up her room and see that she was comfortable. He was instructed to wait outside for the medic who would wheel her stretcher inside. Catherine entered that rehab alone. Michael had explained this to her, but he wasn't sure how much she understood. How could she? She'd been hallucinating on and off during the previous weeks, and COVID-19 was difficult for everyone to comprehend. We were horrified by this turn of events, and we were helpless. Catherine was on her own. Imprisoned. It was clear that for the foreseeable future there'd be no more visits—even from her son! It was heartbreaking.

UNTHINKABLE

2020

My son cups a rose
that has fallen.
"Do boys die too
or just old people?"

COVID-19 CONTINUED TO ACCELERATE, AND NEW YORK CITY became the epicenter in the United States. All nonessential businesses closed. We were all quarantined at home. The onslaught of grief intensified. There could be no memorial service for Catherine. None of us would be present to accompany her on this last journey. We abandoned her. We had no choice, but we abandoned her all the same. Now each of us who loved her walks this loss alone.

I am still haunted by the image of her by herself in a dark room, waiting for the cremation that would scorch her body to ashes. It is all I see when I wake in the middle of the night. Cremation was Catherine's choice—she refused to have Michael bear the expense of a casket burial—even though, to me, cremation seems too severe, too cruel an end.

Therapist Joan responds:

> Such incredible distance between what the mind registers and the fact that she is not her body anymore.

True, burial seems like the more loving, tender dissolution of the body. Yet that's an issue for those of us who survive the death of a loved one, not for the one who has ceased to be.

And where is she? Some say in heaven, some believe her soul is in another life, even species. Others say that death is the end—there is no next stage. This is the answer I fear most, and the one I believe is most likely. The life we loved no longer exists in any form. Catherine doesn't exist in any form. How is this possible? How could she be gone? She'd been here for almost eighty-two years and now she isn't?

We'd just spent back-to-back days and weeks with her. David, Alan, Michael, Maureen, Dolores, and I had wrapped our frighteningly ill Catherine in gentle hugs and kisses, jokes, laughter, and reassurances for three months. And now she just . . . *isn't*. Such a harsh way God has of treating his family, taking Catherine away in an instant.

No, not away. Erasing her. At whim. Where's the humanity in that? A life that struggled to make its way into the world, which took nine months' preparation and eighty-two years of nuts-and-bolts hard living, wiped out. How's that for exerting control?

I sound angry.

I am.

CHAINED

1975

Years fall
like heavy
boots, press
into the earth, leave
patterns
in dust.

THE DEATH OF CATHERINE TRIGGERED A RETURN TO THE CHURCH, after thirty years of separation. These events are intimately connected with religious beliefs—death and afterlife, the essence of God, sin.

Once a very devout Catholic, whose faith in God and the Church was virtually indestructible, I no longer believe. In the Church. In God, yes, sadly even Him. A glimmer from time to time—a sense of something more—but nothing to sustain me. Faith, the firm belief that God was listening to my prayers, had always buttressed me through the worst of days—the boys screaming in the alley, my height, the boils, Mom on the warpath switching from loving to fury. I knew the Lord answered some prayers but not others, that He needed us to suffer longer, so we could help release more souls from purgatory to heaven. Praying was my way of talking about everything with the Lord and of finding solace and hope in His love. He was my friend. My most important friend. Another dad. Always listening. I had a heavenly family watching out for me and protecting me, and since union with the Lord was guaranteed for a life well lived, I feared death less. Afterlife was the greater life, the Church said. I would spend eternity with the Lord. As would my loved ones. Living without Him is a great loss, particularly now when I'm mourning the loss of Catherine and feeling out of control in the other parts of my life. When my faith was strong, I never felt alone. Now I do.

I was twenty-nine years old when I separated from my first husband and was on the way to a divorce, which was not recognized in the Church. According to Catholic doctrine, I was married to this man for life and could not consider marrying again without fear of excommunication.

I didn't want a divorce, but my ex insisted. His girlfriend was pregnant and didn't know he was married, and his only resolution to that conundrum was to marry her. Those were the days when religion—particularly the Catholic Church—controlled our lives and dictated our choices. Sex outside of marriage was anathema—a mortal sin, punishable by damnation for eternity. The only conceivable way to right such a wrong was to marry the girl if she was pregnant.

That's what my ex chose to do, and he wanted my cooperation. I should go to Juarez, Mexico—famous for its speedy divorces attained in a matter of two or three days—to secure a divorce, so he could remarry. Immediately! He told me this late one Sunday afternoon when he returned home after a night "out with the boys" and a day and a half spent who-knows-where. It had become his pattern. He would disappear for entire weekends.

A constant swagger in his hips and attitude, Tom was smooth and had won me over with his impenetrable confidence four years before. I have never met anyone who was so uninterested in what others thought of him. Sandy hair, ruddy complexion, thick build, and tall. He looked like a typical Irishman—from Kerry, in fact, the same county in Ireland as my mother and Dr. O'Leary. Wherever he went, he drew a crowd and plenty of laughter at his sarcastic jokes targeting whomever or whatever was his victim of choice. Like Sonny and the boys in the alley. He never finished high school but he wore my college ring, which convinced everyone that he was a college graduate. He quit several jobs—bartending, construction, insurance salesperson. Undaunted, I was simply in love and mesmerized by a man who seemed to adore me. Fearless, he was all bravado, and that spelled strength to me. One night he came home drunk (he'd never had a drink until he married me, he often bragged), wearing a Green Beret cap and accompanied by the soldier whose hat he had commandeered at the local bar. He swaggered around the house, flaunting the beret while I trembled at the thought that he'd gone too far this time. You didn't steal the hat of a Green Beret and survive.

I was too frightened to go back to bed and leave the two of them. When would the Green Beret decide to take back his cap? These guys were mercenaries! I imagined blood and fists flying as the two of them fought it out in the middle of our pristine living room—between the hand-painted vase, blush silk pillows, and velvet couch. I made bacon and eggs for the two of them and kept them talking and drinking strong coffee until sun broke, reminding the Green Beret that he was expected home hours earlier. Tom removed the hat and returned it peacefully to its rightful owner who jovially said, "Thanks for breakfast," to me and "Good to meet you—you should sign up," to Tom.

Despite my attractiveness to men, I was still very innocent, and Tom had been my first serious boyfriend. With him, I felt like a queen. I was sure I couldn't live without him. I was so frantic I offered to adopt his girlfriend's baby. Such desperation! It still shames me. He refused to raise the child as our own and I refused to accompany him to Juarez for a divorce. His solution: he married her in Church a few weeks later.

He never attempted a divorce himself. When I was ready, I divorced him. But not in Juarez. In a New York City-Bronx court. And now that I was Joan Cusack again, the Church said I could not remarry. I was still married. For Life.

I struggled with this injustice for months. The Jesus I knew was not to blame. He would not sentence me to a life without love, without family. His heart was too pure for that. He wouldn't want to see me alone for the rest of my life. I had entered this marriage honestly and remained faithful throughout. I didn't deserve to remain chained to this man who had betrayed me and our vows. This wasn't what I saw for my life.

I grew more and more disenchanted with the Church—this beacon of perfection and love. I doubted its integrity. Life was not black and white. There had to be room for compassion. Mine was a loving God. The Church's was withholding. Cruel.

PEACE BE WITH YOU

1970

THE LAST MASS I ATTENDED ON MY OWN OCCURRED TOWARD THE end of my first marriage. Though I lived in Lincoln Park, New Jersey, on that Sunday, I chose to go to Mass at the Bronx church I grew up in and my parents still attended, St. Frances de Chantal. It had been my home all my young life, and I trusted the priests (and nuns in the attached school), especially Father Jordan, the recently retired pastor with a heart that fit Jesus. If any place was safe, it was there.

Pope John XXIII had decreed that the language of the country in which Mass was celebrated should be the language of the Mass, except in special circumstances. This marked a significant departure from the traditional Latin, the language of Catholicism from the earliest days of the Church. Instead, Pope John had opened the Mass and Church services to contemporary music—sung and played by church members! Guitars became part of the ritual. At the center of these changes was the offering of the Sign of Peace. Until then, people were not permitted to speak in church except to say the prayers along with the priest. With the introduction of the Sign of Peace, Pope John introduced a sense of community to the Mass. People were invited to offer each other the Sign of Peace in the form of a handshake and the words, "Peace be with you."

Though many traditional conservative Catholics were unhappy with the changes, most were enthusiastic. Mass became a place of joy and contact between parishioners. The stiffness and provincialism that had been part of the church experience was gone, and a warm camaraderie replaced it. Yet at that Mass, there was no Sign of Peace. I was upset and spoke to Father Halpern, the new pastor who had taken Father Jordan's place. When I asked him why the Sign of Peace was absent, he told me it wasn't required by the Vatican, so he made the choice to not include it in the masses at St. Frances. I couldn't believe it. Why would he refuse to offer his parishioners the gift of community?

When I raised the issue of my marital status with him, he underscored that should I marry again, I'd be excommunicated from the Church. I was shattered. How could he say no to his parishioners and yes to this archaic rule banning me from the Church?

Raising his voice, he reiterated his truth: "If you marry again, you are forbidden to participate in or partake of any of the sacraments. You are no longer a member of the Catholic Church!"

Looking back, I question my decision to confide in this staunchly conservative priest.

Therapist Joan challenges me:

> What did you expect? Clearly, he was the wrong person to have approached with a plea for compassion. For flexibility. Under normal circumstances, you would have known that, but you had repressed it. Why? I have to conclude that unconsciously you were looking to him to confirm your belief that the Church had no room for you. In a sense, he made the decision for you.

The vision of this arrogant man represents all that I rejected about the Church. I did not wait for the Church to ban me. I left on my own.

ALL THAT MATTERED

1990

Now the night takes over,
draws strange lines
on our faces.

THE HARDEST PART OF BREAKING WITH THE CHURCH WAS TELLING my father. I knew that this news would break his heart. On the one hand, he was adept at making room for what he couldn't change. On the other, he was a staunch believer and expected me to accept the Church's teachings. Yes, he was saddened, too, that at twenty-nine I wouldn't be able to start a family, but that's where faith comes in. The Church's teachings were the final authority. What it said was gospel. One had no choice but to obey. What God hath joined together, let no man put asunder.

But despite this major shift in our beliefs, my father still embraced me. And I him. Though I no longer went to Mass myself, I accompanied him when he visited for weekends in East Hampton.

"Maybe someday, Honey, you'll come by yourself," he said tenderly as we walked to the car one Sunday morning. I think we were holding hands. He didn't say, "Someday, I hope you'll return. It would make me so happy. I pray for it every day," which would have seared me with guilt each time I thought of him. To protect myself from the guilt, I'd have likely repressed thoughts of him.

Instead, I'm free to answer lightly, as I did that day, "Maybe, I will." And maybe that's true. I'd love to wake up one day and feel like going to Mass again. I'm sure I'd feel my father there.

The miracle of my parents, particularly my father, was their ability to change. To adjust to a reality that was foreign to them. Over the years, I remained open with them. They knew my struggle. My mother advocated for me with Dad. She had no ambivalence about my right to remarry. What she wanted for me was love, and her allegiance to the Church did not compete. Dad and I valued our friendship, and he made many adjustments over the ensuing years for that closeness to be possible. I filed for a divorce. When I remarried, the man was Jewish; we were married in a civil ceremony; and our son was Bar Mitzvahed, like his father. Not surprisingly, I did not pursue a Church annulment. To do so would have required that I claim I had made the vows of my first marriage dishonestly. I didn't believe that and chose not to lie. I knew the truth. That was all that mattered.

REGRETS

2020

Above us,
the moon
holds on
to what it
has left

IN THE MIDST OF QUARANTINE, I CONTINUE TO OBSESS OVER THE injustice that Catherine endured in her lifetime and in her untimely death. Forced quarantine allows for no relief from grief. Other than Alan, there is little to distract me—the girls, David, and Marlene are hunkered down in Florida at Marlene's mom's farm and save for a weekly FaceTime call, we have no contact with them. There's relief in knowing that they're safe (as much as anyone is safe in this threatening time), and luckily they are with their parents and grandma, entertained by the chickens and other natural gifts that living on a farm offers. Remarkably, the incidence of COVID is virtually nonexistent in their rural community—a great blessing for them and for us. So, I spend my days thinking about Catherine and the painful series of events that marred her life—the most painful being the distance from our mother.

Catherine was devoted to Mom and never missed their morning call, when they'd chat about the day ahead. As I focus now on Catherine's losses, I'm struck by how unfair life can be, how broken our family feels, with our two brothers gone from our lives since Dad's death. Catherine had spoken to Dad daily as she did with Mom and attended to all his business and financial needs while he cooked and baked the bread after Mom died. Clearly, Catherine was the most faithful of the four of us. I managed biweekly calls to our parents, our brother Jerry called even less, and Sonny could be counted on for an annual call to Dad, during which they reminisced about their time working together before Sonny's accident. Catherine deserved more.

Fortunately, she had her son who lived with her during the week and tended to her immediate needs—like taking her to the doctor, going to the pharmacy, and shopping for food. Besides Michael, her faith sustained her for her lifetime until this most serious illness. Her faith remained strong and her trust in the Blessed Mother and the Lord were intact. She trusted her heavenly family and turned to them in times of loneliness and need.

In a very real way, our brothers and Mom abandoned her. As did I. She is more alive to me now than she was in life when my resentment of her dependency consumed our relationship. Though my chest heaves with regret, I am grateful that quarantine has allowed room in my life to focus on Catherine; her goodness; her devotion to Mom, Dad, our family, and her son; and her eagerness to please—even her unresponsive siblings.

After I left the Church, I wondered if I'd ever regret my decision. I was still raw with the possibility that I might be committing an unspeakable sin. Yet I did it—despite my terror that I had gone too far this time. Now, forty years since, I do not regret that choice. I never have, and that surprises me somewhat. I was so young, barely twenty-nine, yet I stand behind my choice to this day. I've never wavered.

I was uncomfortable with the Church's rigidity. It's lack of compassion and flexibility. So foreign from the Jesus I was brought up on—the gentle, forgiving Jesus who didn't reject Mary Magdalene, but in kindness, embraced her, washed her feet. Blind faith was required by the Church, and too much in life required openness and thoughtfulness. The older and more educated I became, the deeper was my conviction. Why would God create us with the capacity to think and yet require that we reject that gift in favor of blind acceptance of the dictates of the Church?

Apart from my guilt about my insensitive, cold response to Catherine's complaints, there's actually very little that I regret about the decisions I've made in my life—including my first marriage, my divorce, remarriage, decision to have a child, my many careers. All evolved naturally from the circumstances of my life and my emotional and psychological state at the time. I cannot regret a decision that flowed inevitably from my history and developmental age. During my first marriage, I was emotionally damaged, inexperienced, and vulnerable to the man who claimed to love me beyond measure. Rather than regret my marriage, I was left with incredible shame that I had been so blinded by the need for his love.

My subsequent decisions represented varying degrees of emancipation and rebirth as I made my way toward discovering who I was, what I needed, what I owed myself. When Tom left, I made a vow that I would never consciously expose myself to such pain and rejection again. I would train myself to set off a red light in my head anytime I considered opening myself up to anyone like him. Ten years (and several men) following my divorce, I met my beloved Alan, now with an increased awareness of who I was and who I could be.

My next step was to start psychotherapy treatment. That was the beginning of my forty-year commitment to therapy and my own wellness. It was my first clear awareness of my need and responsibility to self-parent. Therapy was critical for my growth, but it wasn't enough. Change required ongoing, conscious work. I continue to repair the damage I sustained in my early life through creative expression and inward reflection and now, through writing this memoir. Interestingly enough, the more I wrote, the more I remembered. Whole rooms opened, revealing events, people, circumstances, and feelings that I had repressed.

My regrets have more to do with the people in my life and my lack of attention to them. The saddest of these is my refusal to accept my

Dad's vulnerability as he aged—his diminished confidence just prior to his death and not joining him for afternoon walks in East Hampton. I regret not calling him, my mother, and Catherine more often, as well as not recognizing how lonely David was as a child. I regret not recognizing my mother's generosity and commitment to bring me into adulthood, unashamed and resilient; I regret not standing up to her when she belittled Catherine; I regret taking Alan for granted and not partnering with him enough on household responsibilities; I regret not being present to some friends in time of need. Some of these I can no longer change. For those that I can, I try to keep them present in my mind.

BEREFT

Ongoing

Inside this room,
only the sound of
our bodies rocking.

WHILE I DON'T REGRET MY DECISION TO LEAVE THE CHURCH, I'M sad that it was necessary. I loved being Catholic. Growing up, I was proud and grateful to be part of the "one true religion" I learned about in Catechism class. When I believed in an afterlife and a reunion with the Lord, I feared death less. As a younger person, I craved isolation, which I associated with freedom. Now isolation reflects the endless, eternal isolation of death. Without my devotion, I can't seem to reassure myself that once dead, I will not feel so alone. I will not feel anything.

I miss believing. It's the loss of being loved unconditionally. Of being held closely and reassured that life does not end. That I'm safe. How desperately I want to believe that! Faith makes it possible to believe that life continues in some grander scheme. That Dad isn't really lost but is living now with God. As is Catherine. Safe in His company rather than being swallowed up by impenetrable dark and nothingness.

What a splendid gift, faith. I'm in God's arms and He's saying that together with me, He holds my loved ones. It makes it possible to believe that there is no such thing as death—a momentary, bodily one, yes, but ultimately we will live on, spiritually united in the communion of saints.

Grieving Catherine's death (and the many seized daily by COVID), I long to believe again in an afterlife. I want all those I love to continue to be. Me included. I want to picture a better life for Catherine, to share Michael's belief that she continues alongside our parents and her husband, maybe even sharing a cigarette. I imagine her sitting on the friendly neighborhood stoop that Heaven must surely provide, The Lord and His Blessed Mother walking over, joining in the fun. She, Mom, and Dad trading wisecracks. Everyone laughing.

Despite our emotional dysfunction, which often sidelined loving instincts and caused each of us considerable pain, there remains such pleasure in belonging to a family that chose laughter as its natural language. While in the hospital, Catherine drew all manner of caregivers—be they doctors, nurses, maintenance people, physical therapists—with her snappy tongue and mildly irreverent jokes. Everyone loved her. They'd never had a patient like her! She'd be popular in heaven. Probably running all the bingo games.

"We need more like her," everyone said when she died. She carried Mom's mantle with grace. They were both as feisty and vibrant as their illnesses would allow.

Try as I might, I have nowhere to place Catherine. I find myself wishing she had treated herself with more care and tenderness, that she had avoided danger and reached new levels of happiness. Maybe she was truly satisfied, happy, as she insisted. It was pure delight to be with her in those light moments.

But I catch myself. My absence of faith devastates me. The loneliness that comes with disbelief leaves me bereft in that child place where I'm afraid, unprotected, alone. As Catherine is unprotected. Like the defenseless doe crouching, whimpering, and trembling on the side of Old Northwest Road last night.

Yesterday, I bought a plain black dress.

III

A House Divided Against Itself

CLOSE WATCH

2019

I STARTED THIS MEMOIR CONCERNED WITH MY INCREASING vulnerability. Catherine's death jerked me into reality about my own aging and mortality. There is danger everywhere. I am slower than I expected to be approaching eighty. COVID quarantine serves my current interests. I don't want to go out. I don't want to see anyone. I don't want to talk. Leave me to my small family.

Still in my nightgown. Almost noon. COVID's raging outside my window, and I can't stop thinking of my sister. The phone rings yet again. Caller ID reads that it's Carol, my closest friend for the past fifty-five years. We have stood together through all the joys and crises that life has brought us. We're sisters of the heart. Talk about everything. But right now, I have no words. I've already ignored so many of her calls, I must answer this one. Knowing her, she'll be worried. She's the toughest person for me to talk to—she knows me better than anyone, except perhaps Alan. There's no way she won't hear the despair in my voice. There's no hiding from her. She knows my soul. Beyond our friendship, Catherine and she were good friends for a while—both shared a love of talking on the phone—catching up, schmoozing, languishing in conversation as if in a warm bath. A luxury I have no patience for. For me, the phone is utilitarian. It makes it possible to break a silence, say hello, share pressing issues, and make plans for an in-person conversation. Put flesh on the bones of our very clipped shorter talks. But that's about it.

Reluctantly, I answer.

"Hi, Sweetheart," she says, her voice soft and concerned, as always.

"Hi," I answer.

"How are you doing?"

"The same," I respond.

To encourage me to talk about what I'm not saying, she mentions guilt: "How terrible guilt is following the loss of a loved one. And so universal."

This triggers a trembling in my chest. The guilt of having precipitated Catherine's death is very raw. I'm not ready to discuss this with anyone but Alan. Lately, he's the only one with whom I have the strength to share my heart. It's just too soon.

"I know you're right, but I can't talk about it now. I will when I can, but not now." I remind myself that I'm not the only one living this hell—painful as it is to accept. I ask how she is faring.

"We're fine," she answers.

"Thanks for calling, Sweetheart. Sorry I can't talk. I'll call when I can."

"No need to apologize. We'll talk when you're ready."

Once the subject of guilt is raised, however, the issue is front and center in my consciousness. Like many devout Catholics, I have suffered from guilt throughout my life. I was never as good a person as I thought I should be. As the Lord wanted. As He deserved, having suffered and died for our sins. I wonder, in fact, why I'm not feeling even more guilt. Therapist Joan reminds me in these moments:

> One of the ways we control the headlong dive into grief is that we modulate how much free association we can handle.

And this is a delicate one. I've been keeping a close watch on what I let in. Guilt was an integral part of my relationship with Catherine. Over the years it plagued me. I knew how important I was to her, and

I wanted to mirror that feeling. I wanted to love her as much as I believed she loved me. But I couldn't. And now it's too late.

I blame my parents and siblings for that. Especially Mom. But it's not the time for pointing fingers. I'll get back to the family's sins. First, I must face my own.

DARK HOUSE

1950s

As a very tall girl with tall parents and three tall siblings, claustrophobia was an often-threatening feeling in my childhood home. Six large people in five tiny rooms was a tight squeeze. There were constant battles—for the bathroom, for space on the couch, for who selected what to watch on TV, who got the larger dollop of mashed potatoes, the last piece of cake. When tensions grew taut, there were dark days—Mom descended into her dark moods or Sonny revved up for more taunting.

Afternoons he'd be there waiting
finishing his tea and jellied toast.
He wouldn't even let me take off
my coat, throwing me down on
the bed, daring me to try to
get up. With the tips of his fingers
between my breasts, he'd jab me
and knock me down again.

Catherine and Mom regularly retold a story about Sonny sneaking me into a closet and cutting off all my thick, waist-length curls. He was five and I was four.

"You looked like a boy when he was finished," Mom said.

Everyone in the family remembered it besides Jerry and me. I can only surmise how terrified I felt; it's not a surprise that I couldn't recall the incident. Where were Mom and Dad? Didn't someone see us disappearing into the closet in a house so small? Was Sonny punished? How did I react when he was finished? What did I look like? Did we all sit around the kitchen table for dinner just like normal? What did we talk about? I never asked Catherine or Mom those questions, though on occasion I try to picture the scene, imagining Dad and Mom being righteously angry, punishing Sonny, protecting me. And it's important to me to know whether Catherine laughed. But for some reason, I could never ask her.

Whenever she would bring up the incident, I'd say, "I don't remember and don't want to talk about it—I don't want any details."

Reflecting on this story, Therapist Joan says:

> You know what's going on. You don't remember because you psychologically defended yourself from having to experience the trauma again. This is the way our psyche works. It eliminates a memory from our conscious mind and 'stores' it in the unconscious.

To her analysis, I answer, "While what you're saying is true, I now realize that while I didn't want any details of the assault while Mom and Catherine were alive, I do want them now."

The hair-cutting incident was a perfect example of the family dynamic when everyone would have shown their true colors. It's likely that Catherine laughed at ugly me, and that Mom and Dad didn't punish Sonny. That no one in the family took care of me. Everyone knew I was Sonny's toy. Nothing pleased him more than scaring the daylights out of me with strange and ominous sounds coming from the cellar or fearsome shadows lunging from my bedroom wall. I was the perfect victim, afraid to fight or protect myself. I just tried to stay out of his way and "make nice" when he caught up with me. In five tiny rooms, there wasn't much space to hide.

There were days I'd lie there,
refuse to get up but he'd threaten
to punch me if I didn't obey
my Big Brother, huge in the
doorway, all juiced up

Catherine and our younger brother Jerry eventually joined Sonny, targeting me as Mom's favorite, since she didn't take the belt to me. The way I shook in terror whenever I was in trouble seemed to be sufficient punishment. Then one day she came home from work to what she called *Bedlam.*

Jerry was stretched out lengthwise on the piano, and Sonny was jumping from the couch to Dad's chair, yelling, "The bigger they are, the harder they fall!"

"I'm the mother when mother is out!" Catherine shouted repeatedly, but to no avail.

I called out, "Mom'll be home any minute! We'll get the strap!" when suddenly she appeared in the doorway raging.

"You'll get the strap, all right!" as she grabbed it from its place on the coat rack and started wielding it—at the boys mostly, but at me and Catherine, too!

I was trembling, begging, "Please Mom don't hit me. I didn't do anything. I tried to stop them."

"Stop the shaking or you'll get it worse," she bellowed. But I couldn't be still; my whole body was in a frenzy. She was convinced I was faking and screamed, "Now you'll get the same treatment as the other three."

And so, I did. The skin on my back and arms were on fire from the belt. The trembling lasted into the night. To this day, I still don't know if and how much of my shaking was staged to keep me from the belt. But I didn't feel like her favorite. I certainly never felt safe.

Me rocking up and down on the bed,
the cold rush of pee and the dark stain
of shame spreading through my uniform.

The worst sibling retribution to my memory involved Mom, Catherine, and Sonny. In constant fear of committing a sin or angering Mom, I always followed her commandments that she, home, and family came first. Catherine ignored most of her demands. Friends came first. What was considered normal adolescent behavior was aberrant to Mom. Then one day, she insisted that I spy on Sonny and Catherine after school and report back to her if they were smoking.

I froze. When I begged to please not have to do it, she insisted she needed my help. It was my job.

"You're the only one I can count on," she said. "Jerry's too young."

Terrified, I obeyed. Such betrayal! One that almost destroyed my relationship with Sonny, who still flies into a rage when the topic of me snitching comes up. Fortunately, Cath forgave me (at least I think she did). It's no surprise that I dreamed of freedom—buying a car and taking off as often as I could to as many places as possible.

SELFISH

1958 / 2015

GROWING UP, CATHERINE WAS MY COOL OLDER SISTER. I WAS crazy about her. I wanted to be her friend, but I knew I didn't measure up. She just couldn't have a younger, lankier sister hanging out with her. The "crowd" would lose respect. I didn't resent her for that. I told myself she had no choice. It didn't hurt if I pretended that was true. So, I pushed my wish for closeness away.

There were four and a half years' difference in age between us, which amounts to at least a generation when you're kids. Our interests were also different. She loved sports and played on the basketball team. I loved reading. I had only two or three close girlfriends. She had many, who were all the cool kids in school and the neighborhood—boys and girls who hung out together at the local candy store and Sandy Beach and traveled in a pack. Not surprisingly, Catherine and I headed in different directions for high school. She went to St. Catherine's School of Business to be a secretary, the profession of choice for most Edgewater girls. I, to Preston, our local academic school.

As an adult, Catherine walked through her life. I, on the other hand, ran. The difference in our pace and our interests made constant tension between us. Catherine's early friendships remained consistent throughout her life, while I had varied relationships over the years, which ebbed and flowed based on my writing, professional work, and social life.

Catherine was satisfied to remain close to home. I traveled every time I could put two weeks together and have toured extensively through Europe, Asia, Africa, South America, and the US. There was so much to see! I wanted to know what was on the other side of the horizon. To go on safaris, see glaciers, oceans, mountains. Catherine showed no interest in travel other than a visit to Austria, her second husband's birthplace, and Ireland with our parents. She never really left Edgewater. I couldn't wait to get out.

Catherine never drove, though she had a license. She wasn't ready, she said. A perfectionist, she insisted on doing everything in perfect order, whether it meant dusting the hangers in her closet or, when we were kids, rescouring the tub after I'd finished because she wasn't satisfied that it was clean until she gave it "The Catherine Look." When we were in school, she laid out her clothes every night—her perfectly washed, ironed, and folded uniform and blouse on the chair by her bed made such a lovely picture each morning.

Catherine's perfection sharply contrasted with my mess. Our bedroom was the embodiment of a psychotic episode. "Collier's Mansion," Mom called it. On my side of the room, I pushed yesterday's clothes (and the days' before) to the side to get into bed. Why put them away? I'd be wearing them again later in the week. I imagine it was horrifying for Catherine to live with a sister who was such a slob (my word)! But she didn't complain. Mom took care of that.

I worried about Catherine being alone. As a teenager, I thought a lot about why Mom seemed to love me and not her. Dad always had a special place in his heart for Catherine, but he kept out of the fray rather than incite Mom's jealousy. Of the four of us, three could do no wrong. Catherine could do no right. Mom criticized her friends, her lack of loyalty, her husbands, her clothes. My heart ached for my sister during those years, and I deeply resented Mom for her abuse. Yet I didn't confront her. Challenging her was forbidden—she accepted no input that didn't align with her position and flew into a rage when anyone disagreed with her, even Dad. The best I could do was say nothing, like he did.

Though I stated earlier that I have few regrets in my lifetime, I profoundly regret this. In my forty years of therapy, I never focused on it.

Saying it now forces me to admit it. I was terrified of Mom. We all were. Which meant Catherine was on her own.

The image of my isolated sister entering the rehab center on the first day of quarantine and the last day of her life underscores my devastation. The thought of her alone in that dark room waiting for cremation crushes me. I want to put my arms around her. But I couldn't—not when she was alive or when she was dead. This shames me.

Sadly, Catherine and I were never in sync, and I can't remember a time when I didn't feel guilty about that. As aging adults, our relationship was marred by my not being able to return her love. She finally wanted us to be best friends—considered us so—but I seldom felt close to her. We never truly understood each other. I didn't need her as she needed me to. I had already created my own family—Alan, David, his daughters, Cassidy and Elodie, my niece Aimeé, my good friends Carol, Charlene, Karen, and Teresa, Alan's cousin Maida and her three adult daughters, Monica, Pamela, and Carol, and my community of writers—all who embraced me as I was.

Catherine's dependence on me became increasingly more difficult after her second husband died, which perpetuated my ongoing resentment, anger, and guilt. After Michael, I was her first call when she was in crisis. The roof was leaking, the shower didn't function, or she had a medical or financial emergency. The practical things were relatively easy. Alan and I had been contributing to her income monthly and took care of house repairs as they came up. But the medical issues were difficult to manage. I offered the usual suggestions and asked predictable questions. Had she spoken to her doctor as she said she would? Why not call the pharmacy and have her prescription delivered? But her answers were equally familiar. She said she would follow up, but never did. The next time we spoke, the problem was the same. I came to dread those calls.

In the end, I felt responsible for relieving her suffering. Despite my height-related stress, the boils, fusions, separation from the Church, and ongoing depression, nothing measured up to Catherine's painful rejection by Mom. She felt that Mom preferred me over her. And the truth in this made it all the more painful.

SIBLINGS

Ongoing

MY DREAM FOR AS LONG AS I CAN REMEMBER WAS TO ATTEND college (I was literally the first girl in Edgewater to do so) and prepare for a teaching career. I was considered the "smart one" in the family. Jerry, too. We both went to St John's and earned PhDs in psychology from NYU. We were a team and planned to open a joint psychology practice together when we finished our degrees. Those were special years, sharing our clinical challenges and supporting each other during our earliest years when we were most vulnerable about the intense career path that we had chosen.

As children, Jerry and I were always together. I took care of him, played with him, and made sure he got everything he wanted. Well, what I imagined he wanted, which was usually what I wished for as a child but didn't get.

Mom made sure we had colored eggs for Easter, but we didn't have individual baskets, so I decided that I'd make one for Jerry. It was the biggest Easter basket either of us had ever seen. I paid for it with weeks of babysitting money. It was so lovely shopping for all the goodies I'd include—jellybeans, chicks, chocolate bears, bunnies, fake grass that I hid the treats in. He loved it, and I was overjoyed to give it to him.

For a brief few years before rekindling our closeness in college, we made our own friends at school and we drifted apart. It's strange that I don't remember missing him, but I must have. I want to believe we missed each other. Once again, after college we drifted apart again, then came together when we opened our practices. We repeated this pattern several times over the years—the last time was after Dad's funeral over ten years ago. Neither of us has pursued a retrieval of that friendship after that, except for once several years ago. Out of the blue he sent me a very beautiful Mary Oliver poem, "The Wild Thing," and surprised me with a phone call to give me the name of a doctor he had great faith in. Periodically, I wonder why I haven't pursued a reconnection with him, especially after his two generous gestures.

Therapist Joan suggests:

> It would seem that you can't take the risk of him disappearing again . . . a predictable and very painful loss that would stem from poor judgment on your part. At this point in your life your focus is on your own well-being and that of your immediate family and faithful girlfriends.

So, too, Catherine and Sonny were a team. They were not ambitious professionally, even though Mom went to work at Catholic Charities as a home care worker to save for their tuition, just as she saved for Jerry's and mine. But they weren't interested. I often wondered if Mom resented them for that, though I don't recall her showing it. Their goals took them to good jobs after high school, which provided them with decent living wages—most parents' main concern at that time. Catherine worked as a secretary for the chair of the English Department at NYU and Sonny as a plumber, working side by side with Dad.

But that partnership was short lived. As soon as he could save enough money, Sonny bought a motorcycle and took a trip to Mexico with his biker friends. Regrettably, on his way back, he was severely injured, his arms and legs broken, and several bones in his back. That was a major catastrophe in our family. He spent six months in a hospital in South Boston, Virginia. Devastated, Mom and Dad drove the eight hours back and forth every weekend to be with him. When he returned to New York, he remained bedridden in a full body cast and was cared for by Mom for the better part of a year. A profound imprisonment for them—literally for Sonny and metaphorically for my parents. Though we never talked about it, it makes psychological sense that rage and shame would have smoldered in both Mom and Sonny during this time, as their inability to cope with the loss of control that accompanied such a traumatic derailment of their lives and relationship is so alike. But alas, emotional trauma was not attended to in our family. Whatever was smoldering or boiling beneath the surface was left there.

The loneliness they experienced during Sonny's slow recovery must have darkened those days. Remarkably, Sonny, who seemed disconnected from religion and the Church after his altar boy years, turned to reading the Old and New Testaments. He claimed that he never learned to read proficiently in school, so he spent his time immobile working through the text. As is true for many who experience severe challenges of the body, his recovery was a time of transformation. When he came out of the cast, he was unable to return to plumbing work, so he began to focus on art—a gift that was evident since childhood. That became his lifelong focus.

Interestingly enough, both of my brothers are fine artists—Jerry, a sculptor and Sonny, a painter. Jerry is also a gifted singer who sang for all who asked him to. He had two sons, one who grew up to be a Spanish guitarist and teacher and his second, a gifted painter. Though Jerry also demonstrated a natural ability for art as a young boy, next to Sonny's gift, Jerry's didn't measure up. In fact, I don't remember him pursuing art at all until he reached midlife when he discovered sculpting. I recall the day he showed me his first sculpted piece, which everyone said looked just like me. That pleased me—that he thought I was a good subject, that he still felt a closeness to me, but mostly because he had reclaimed art and pursued sculpting. As the younger brother, he often got lost in Sonny's growth as a painter. We all did.

Catherine, meanwhile, had a successful career working first as secretary to the chair of the English Department at NYU and then for Citicorp, where she remained as an executive secretary until she retired. I taught English at two NYC high schools, then went back to school for my master's, and became a guidance counselor before earning my PhD.

Looking back, reflecting on the litany of differences between Catherine and me is likely my way to assuage my guilt for not allowing more closeness between us in our later years. I feel compelled to explain myself—to say it wasn't my fault or to be accusatory—to maintain the distance between us. Her neediness choked me. It began in midlife and lasted until she died. As we aged, she was drastically different from the cool older sister of childhood.

Our conversations usually centered around family and her demand for answers: "You're the psychologist," she'd say. Or "Who else can I ask?" and "What should I do?"

I spent the better half of my life in therapy. Though she often said she'd start, she never did. Therein lies the problem. She figured I'd provide answers, and I resented her refusal to do the work herself. I tried for a while to validate her perceptions (she was right—she had been passed over). After many years of struggling through my own conflicts with family, as well as those of my psychotherapy patients, I couldn't bear to spend our weekly visit discussing her damages and assigning blame. (Ironically, she'd come to my psychology office for these lunch visits.) There was little pleasure in those conversations.

One afternoon in East Hampton, while I was filling the dishwasher and she was sitting at the breakfast table nursing her black coffee and two peanut butter sandwiches, I finally admitted that I wasn't comfortable being her therapist. Digging up the deep, barely acknowledged hurts of our family life was too painful. She felt hurt and saw my reluctance as a rejection.

"You're the expert," she said. "I never went to college, and you know all this stuff." She became very quiet, just sipped her coffee, and after a few minutes, continued clearly annoyed, "Why do I have to go to someone else? You're the professional."

"Catherine, I can't. I was in therapy for over forty years. I can't go back there," I responded.

"You're just selfish," she said, getting up from the table and leaving the room. Painful as it was to hear, I worried that she was right.

When I think back on this conversation, Therapist Joan chimes in:

Keep in mind that for a person like Catherine, putting oneself first was anathema. She didn't see that her refusal to do her own exploration placed a burden on you that you couldn't tolerate emotionally. Perhaps this was a function of her own selfishness—expecting from you what she wouldn't do for herself. You should be able to handle it, she seemed to say. We're sisters, and she had no one else to talk to.

ANOTHER LOOK

1990–2019

My siblings and I never really knew each other. What we knew was surface-level—what we liked to do, who our friends were, did we excel in school. We rarely talked to each other; it never seemed important or relevant. As I look at our lives and accomplishments, I'm struck by how separate we each were, how different, how lonely, I expect. We were given natural gifts—painting and sculpture, writing, voice, intelligence—and followed those as far as we knew how. Our parents, particularly our mother, set us on track—buying a piano and arranging for piano lessons for Catherine and me, providing art lessons for Sonny when he was in fifth grade, and working to pay for college. Beside her, Dad would also accept any moonlighting work he was offered to partner with her in providing us with opportunities that recognized our abilities and interests.

Remarkably, Sonny's fifth grade teacher, Sister Mary Scholastica, was the first one to recognize his talent for art. He wasn't doing well in school, and Sister called for Mom and Dad to speak with them about it. The conversation focused on Sonny's fascination with art. She recounted a day when she was teaching a geography lesson about Mexico and as she walked past Sonny's desk, she noticed that he was drawing a picture of a Mexican farm boy. She was taken by how realistic it was. She recommended that they enroll Sonny in Saturday art classes at Villa Maria Academy close by. What a surprise! The rest of us kids were scared that he'd get a beating when our parents got home. Getting good grades in school was important in our family. But there was no beating. In their conversation with Sonny, they focused only on Sister's recommendation of art classes, and they lost no time in doing so.

It strikes me that over the years I've focused on the dysfunctions of my family and the lack of attention we kids received from our parents. Yet in the process of writing this memoir and zeroing in on the minute details of our lives, I am impressed with how rich a life we led, each of us supported in the quietest way by our parents.

Catherine's wish to leave Preston, our academic high school, was another example. She wanted to transfer to St. Catherine's School of Business. There was no fanfare or bravado, no grueling conversations to convince her that it wasn't something that they could condone or that she was too young to make such a decision. After talking with her about the move, they simply trusted her judgment and made the arrangements for her transfer. And it proved to be the right choice for Catherine. She excelled in business, and she loved it.

This wisdom and flexibility from two people who had very little schooling of their own—Mom's poorly written notes to Sister when we were absent from school showcased this—impresses me. For one who insisted on having her way, Mom was open to Catherine's ability and right to decide for herself what she wanted. A remarkable flexibility for Mom, who was so set in her ways! And a remarkable experience for me now, revisiting a time in our lives when our parents so believed in us. It strikes me that we all followed different paths and in each case our parents supported us and our right to do so.

Even as I write this, a quiet but profound pleasure accompanies this awareness. Our parents loved us. Each of us. And they believed in us.

Therapist Joan concurs:

> How vital a resource is this unlayering of our early lives and gifts. Once again, your need to repress your anger and the guilt that went with it has forced you into a closet that has remained locked until now. How vast are the joys that you can embrace now that you have

opened your unconscious to the riches that lay hidden for so long. How potent a method of unveiling a source of your depression.

It's true. I always assumed that my wanderlust was an innate part of myself. Reflecting on the lives of my siblings and our parents' support underscores how much we were influenced by them. Subtle influence but powerful enough to quietly guide us to become the hardworking talented people that we became, from Jerry's singing, to Sonny's painting, and my self-confidence to speak my mind. Jerry was encouraged to sing for the neighbors, particularly Mr. Shadel, the police detective who lived next door and taught all four of us Cusack kids to dive, and Mr. O'Shea, an Irishman from down the street who was a great fan of Jerry's singing.

Mom and Dad invited me to speak my mind to adults I didn't agree with—like Julia, the Irish lady who lived behind us, who constantly complained about the state of this country to me while she was sweeping her yard and I was hanging out the laundry. I got tired of hearing how difficult things were for her and her husband and, one day, snapped.

"Well, maybe you should move back to Ireland if you're not happy here."

Mom and Dad just laughed. As long as I wasn't disrespectful, they saw nothing wrong with my directness. I'm convinced that permission gave me the confidence to trust in my voice and self-agency. They respected our choices, and those choices influenced the people we became, including our values of honesty, generosity, charity, and humanity. A prime example was Sonny's refusal to sue the woman who hit him on his motorcycle. The sheriff on the scene told Dad he was thrown twenty-five feet over the hood of her car. The lawyers who showed up at Sonny's bedside offering to represent him regarded his as "a sure win" and "a very strong" case. Sonny adamantly refused. Her only asset was her farm, and he would not leave her destitute. I'm very proud of his generosity.

BROTHERS ESCAPE

1980 / 2022

Despite the aforementioned riches, there is more to the sagas of my brothers, particularly Sonny. Both have been estranged from the family for decades. Jerry left after Dad's funeral—he broke off with me and Catherine, too, after a disagreement that turned bitter between his wife and me. Sonny left much earlier. He and my parents had a tumultuous relationship for most of his life. He was the rebel of the family and did what he wanted, irrespective of the rules of the house. Mom's rules.

After he recovered from his motorcycle accident, he married, had two daughters, and moved to Mexico, devoting himself entirely to painting. In the small artist community of San Miguel de Allende, where he settled, the similarity of his painting style to Rembrandt's earned him the name El Padron and considerable success painting huge murals for the Catholic Church. His return to the United States spelled a series of conflicts, when he and his family moved in with our parents in their undersized house, the one we grew up in. Mom and Sonny, two volatile personalities, made for an unstable household until he moved out and settled first in Brooklyn, then in England. Their relationship calmed, and soon Mom and Dad began visiting him in Brooklyn while Jerry took over as his business manager, overseeing his New York gallery shows. At one point, I too got involved and organized and hosted a show for him in my New Jersey home, selling several thousand dollars in paintings. We were all at one point or another devoted to his work and to him, and we financially supported both, so that he could continue to paint and not have to worry about making a living. With his wife's job and family help, they managed quite nicely.

But over time, he became explosive and contemptuous of all of us (except Catherine). He finally broke off relationships permanently when we did not abide by his command to exclude his daughters (both of whom had left home, despite his resistance) in our family Christmas celebration. He demanded that we choose him or his daughters. We chose Maureen and Dolores.

That was the end of contact between Sonny and the rest of the family. He refused to come to our mother's funeral but attended Dad's, though he was gone again immediately after. That said, despite his absence, he came twice to the hospital to see Catherine during her final months. She was the one person in our family that he never displayed contempt for. They were a team from childhood, both always in trouble with Mom. It was Catherine who signed for Sonny's motorcycle when Mom and Dad refused. They were furious with her, but she was steadfast.

Though Sonny remained faithful to Catherine, Jerry and Dot had little contact with her. They had many friends and entertained them at their home, always extending an invitation to me. Catherine never received the same invitations (though I never told her, she always found out), and she was hurt that she remained on the outside and I was on the inside. And I did little to nothing about it. But what could I have done? Not attended the parties? Maybe. Suggested that they invite her? But who was I to tell Jerry and Dot who to invite to their home? I did, however, make it my business to host holiday family gatherings and always included her. That was one way I compensated.

Sadly, despite Sonny's love, Catherine's life as she aged remained solitary. Divorced from her first husband, Michael's father, she remarried. Far from a loving husband, her second was as critical and controlling as Mom. Though her friends and I urged her to leave him, she would not. He was on disability and depended on her. She vowed for better or for worse. In sickness and in health. She would live out her life with him. And so, she did until he died several years later. It was then that her dependency on me increased, and soon after, she fell ill herself.

RESENTMENT DEEPENS, GUILT FESTERS

2010 / 2020

CATHERINE HAD MULTIPLE MAJOR MEDICAL SCARES OVER THE years. Michael and I were with her for each hospital or rehab stay, accompanying her for tests and doctor's appointments, pleading with her to try harder to treat herself well, to eat healthy meals, and to give up smoking. Though we knew she wouldn't.

What Michael couldn't do, I did. I was her sister. How could I not? My resentment deepened. Along with my guilt. I regretted (but could not control) the grumpiness I expressed when I was with her. It was hard to resist chastising her over the many behaviors that frustrated me. We were a team: she provoked, I flailed. We walked into the same glass wall for the last twenty years.

Typically, Catherine would close the door to the pulmonologist's office, take a cigarette out of her pocket, and light up. Then she'd head for the car where I was waiting. Despite the darkening sky and the imminent threat of a storm, she moved painfully slowly, as if she were absorbing each precious moment of a bright sunny day. She had a narrow window to enjoy her cigarette before stubbing it out on the pavement and returning it to her pocket before getting into the car. Cigarettes cost money. Catherine didn't waste them. She knew how much I hated seeing her smoking, but it didn't seem to faze her. I was saving her the hassle of having to take public transportation—why couldn't she reciprocate by not smoking in front of me?

"I wasn't doing it in front of you, I was a half a block away," she snapped.

"What's the point?" I chided myself and changed the topic. "How did it go with the doctor?"

"Fine. My numbers are still the same, 3.5, but she wants to see me monthly, so she can monitor them more closely. As long as I don't go over four, at the most five, I'm safe. More than that and the aneurysm could burst. But right now, I'm fine."

The following morning, while I was relaxing in bed, wrapped in my pink cuddly bathrobe, enjoying my morning coffee, and chatting with Alan who was well on his way to being fully dressed, I filled him in on my frustrating conversation with Catherine.

"She drives me crazy!" I said. "Takes no responsibility for her own health."

"Don't you see that she's limited and can't change?"

Alan's tone and comment infuriated me. This wasn't new. He often chastised me for trying to change her.

"Catherine isn't limited," I snapped. "She's just obstinate! And emotionally arrested."

Thinking back on these conversations, Therapist Joan understands:

> Maybe you just didn't want to see her as limited. You wanted her to be as smart as our brothers and you and capable of assuming responsibility for her life, of treating herself like she loved and valued herself.

But perhaps I was afraid that wasn't true. And the terror of my own aging was exacerbated by watching her decline. Was this what was waiting for me? It seemed like she had given up. Yet she claimed she had a good life and felt optimistic. I wanted to believe her. I'd accept what she said and wouldn't call her for a few weeks, guilt smoldering. Well, at least we weren't fighting. Alan and David had made their point. I could not change her.

"Let her be, Mom. Just try to enjoy your time with her," David insisted.

He means well, I thought. But the battle wasn't his, and she wasn't his sister. Enjoy? How could I find enjoyment in her stubbornness? Yet I knew he and Alan were right. Everything I understood professionally told me I was on a collision course.

PEACE, FINALLY

2020

I WAS THE FIRST AND ONLY MEMBER OF MY FAMILY TO GET COVID. I was feeling quite ill—weak, bad headache, exhaustion, fever, sleeping for long hours. Alan took me to the local urgent care and that confirmed it. I had hoped not to get sick and burden Alan and David (who was back with his family from Florida) with my care, but here I was again—sick, dependent, and feeling helpless. Alan put on his mask and did all he could—shopping for food, making trips to the pharmacy, and sleeping beside me irrespective of my attempts to convince him to sleep in the other room to avoid getting the virus. He ignored my pleas and never got sick. David was taking care of the girls but took short breaks to check on me. He knew I loved chicken noodle soup, so he brought it to me every day—the only food I could tolerate—and stayed for a brief chat rather than risk contamination of himself and the girls. I was grateful, but guilty too for being a burden once again, and lonely and helpless.

In the two weeks I was sick, I worried about Catherine and was relieved when I learned that she wasn't sick as well. I spent a lot of time thinking about our relationship and eventually decided to free myself of the responsibility to save her. I would let go. No more preaching, no raised voice (always mine—she never talked back, she just incited). It was her life. I would shut my mouth and see if I could muster some peace between us. Get back to laughing as we did so well.

Happily, we managed that during her last several months, especially while she was hospitalized. I remember a particular conversation in which she admitted to being tired and scared about her prolonged hospitalization. Why was it taking so long for the infections to be eliminated? For the pacemaker to be scheduled? For her move to rehab? I told her I admired her strength and resilience in tolerating three months in the hospital in relatively good spirits. I knew I couldn't have done that. I had the luxury of sitting by her bedside and leaving to return to the comfort of my home. She thanked me for saying that. I guess it was hard for her to believe that I would admire her. She was so used to admiring me—her strong baby sister. We each left that conversation feeling a bit better about ourselves. It's a pity that we didn't have more of those talks. It wasn't the only one, but I wish I'd expressed my respect and admiration more often.

And bless us, once I stopped trying to change her, we could finally have light and pleasant conversations. I wasn't angry anymore. Sad, yes, but at peace about my inability to control her. But alas, it never became easy to call. I knew I should be in touch more often and felt guilty for not doing so, but I still resisted until I could live with myself no longer and picked up the phone. Ironically, oftentimes, it would take her another week or two to get back to me. It was a pattern we both followed. So, we were dancing again, still dreading that we'd fall into the same pit. Until guilt pushed us to reach out to each other.

For me, that was usually on a Sunday, late afternoon. I'd be fresh from a nap, having spent a cozy morning with Alan, watching *CBS: Sunday Morning* and *Meet the Press.* I felt sated, rested. It was a natural time for me to reach out. I actually looked forward to hearing her voice. When we finally spoke, we invariably had a friendly conversation—a good sisters' talk about our sons, our favorite topics as moms and aunts. We were crazy about our sons. I kept her up to date with Alan, Cassidy, and Elodie. She shared news on her relentless efforts to find the perfect birthday or Christmas gift for one of the girls. It took her weeks to find and decide on a Flexible Flyer wagon for Elodie like the one we all grew up with. She found a hot pink lavishly tasseled bicycle for Cass. We had a great time emailing links for days, as she shared her thoughtful choices. The girls were thrilled with the wagon and bike.

Moving on from the careful gift giving, I'd ask how she was feeling and tell her how I was feeling. I no longer protected her from knowing that I too had health problems though none were as serious as hers. I told her that I couldn't pick her up and drive her to appointments when we moved to Brooklyn, and she understood and found a local driver who would take over. This was the spirit of our relationship when she was hospitalized for the last time. We were the closest friends we'd ever been. Best friends.

STILL

2022

DESPITE THE FACT THAT CATHERINE AND I REPAIRED OUR DAMaged relationship, her death continues to paralyze me. It pushes against my heart and takes up residence in my shoulder and the small of my back.

It chastises, "You have no more chances." And it threatens, "You're next."

Despite Alan's efforts to entice me to join him for a movie, a ferry ride, or a relaxing break on our terrace to watch the sunset, sadness is my only company. I lie in bed for hours surrounded by my books, cups of coffee, and half-eaten slices of toast. I sleep as many hours as my body will allow. I wanted a better life for her. I wanted to not fail her. Did I? At times I believe I did. I was callous and impatient.

The loss of Catherine coupled with my waning health and increasing years leaves me unsteady and fearful of everything. I wasn't prepared for this. Intellectually, I know that the death of a sibling can bring us shakingly close to our own death. Emotionally, I feel as if I'm being stalked by grief, regret, and time. She was only four years older than me. She was cavalier about her health. I've been cavalier with mine. When I walk now, I'm afraid to look straight ahead, as recommended. I may fall.

Tall me, terrified of falling. Tall. Fall. Only one letter separates them. What will I break this time?

NO ROOM AT THE INN

2019

Around us now, walls of trees—some old,
thick with listening; out there by the road,
a trunk, like a huge cupped hand, twisted
and veined from living on the corner
between two shapes of wind. . . .

"MOM, HAVE YOU THOUGHT ABOUT FINDING SOMEONE TO TALK to?" David asks. He means a therapist.

My response, "I tried. Months ago."

All of my former therapists have died, and it's not so easy to find someone new who is willing to work with a nearly eighty-year-old woman who has forty years of experience working as a psychotherapist and has gone through treatment herself. Perhaps the therapists who reject my inquiries wonder what I have left to discover. Would I have responded the same way if a retired therapist in need of treatment had approached me? I don't think so. My oldest patient was a woman of eighty-four when we began her treatment. True, she wasn't a therapist, but she was a very smart woman who had lots to talk about.

In any case, I need the help of a trained professional as I work my way out of my current depression. I also need to review my medication to ensure if I should continue taking it, at this dose or at all, after all this time. My long-standing pharmacologist passed away, and my primary-care physician has been overseeing prescription renewals.

Maybe this depression is a function of the flood of stressors that are beyond the scope of my current medication. I've been on a maximum dose of antidepressants for more years than I can recall. Our bodies only produce a set amount of the required neurotransmitters irrespective of stress levels and life circumstances. Enter antidepressant medication, which restores the body's chemical balance and makes it possible to do the emotional and psychological work necessary to reduce depression.

My depression predates Catherine's death, COVID, and the sad state of our country. It is connected to my increasing age and physical vulnerability. This is where I was at the beginning of this book. And, in retrospect, probably amplified it.

It was crucial to address the root cause of my falls to prevent further injury. My back was at risk. I had already started making adjustments to reduce the chance of tripping: I took David's advice and shortened my dresses, skirts, and pants, and no longer wore dangling, free-flowing scarves. I also stopped walking barefoot at home and avoided walking anywhere outside without my cane. I carried only a small clutch to hold my glasses and phone. In that way, I tried to take care of my physical needs, but I needed professional help to explore unconscious issues that might be contributing to my falls. The depression deepened with each passing day.

I spoke with a lovely woman at a local psychiatric referral service, and she suggested I make an appointment at the Martha Stewart Center for Living patient outreach facility. Relieved, I did that.

Other trees are sparse, slight as a life
at the bottom. What could be more
fragile, more here for only a moment
but the dogwood . . . so excited
it sprouts shoots all the length
of its frail branches, white

blossoms, wide as a woman
in childbirth, rushing with life
using it up. . . .

According to the message left on my answering machine a few days after my appointment: "There is no one on staff who can provide the services Joan requests."

The message was delivered by an office clerk even though the warm and responsive social worker who interviewed me for a full hour had said she was sure the psychological center could help me and would get back to me herself. What were the services the office couldn't provide? Psychotherapy and medication monitoring were both listed as services they offered. I wasn't invited to participate in the second step of their intake process, which included an interview with a psychiatrist. Why?

Does an aging person stop growing? Do they assume that I'm no longer interested in my mental health just because I'm approaching eighty? Did the social worker feel that I was no longer capable of tackling the psychological rigors of therapy? Or was providing therapy for a person of my age not a worthwhile investment? If that was so, at what age do we become disposable?

What troubles me now is that I didn't pursue the issue any further. I'm known to myself and others as someone who stands up for what I believe, especially my right to fair and respectful treatment. Yet, it was only when I told the story to a close friend and watched disbelief and outrage spread across her face that I questioned the rejection and my response.

I dreaded the thought of returning to therapy at this point in my life. For several years, I had assumed that everything needing attention had been addressed during my forty years as a patient. But I needed help again, and urgently. I was in turmoil. I recognized the signs—extreme sadness, trouble sleeping, emotional disconnection from my husband and son, plagued by terror of my own death. My passivity may also have been a function of my depression and the way I was treated. Not treated. Dismissed.

Hadn't I expressed that to the social worker who interviewed me? Anyone who has experienced an intake knows how stressful, even painful, it can be. I tried to present as complete a picture of who I was and left feeling respected and hopeful. The awkwardness that I felt about making the appointment in the first place was tied to my age and how I might be regarded by the clinicians.

The surprising rejection by the center threw me and exacerbated my feelings of being old and vulnerable. I felt a new urgency to have my medication checked by a psychopharmacologist. I couldn't afford to be defeated by this rejection and needed to turn my attention to finding therapeutic assistance and guidance.

I decided to write a letter to the director of the facility and register a complaint about my shabby treatment. In response to my letter, the facility claimed to not have any record of my interview, which I found deeply disturbing. That said, I decided not to pursue the issue further because it interfered with my focus on pulling myself out of depression. Concentrating on their rejection would only hinder my recovery. And in the meantime, all that was in my power was to continue my writing process to unveil insights and to help me comprehend the sources of my falls and my despair. There were the obvious issues—Catherine's death, my guilt, my own mortality, physical pain, and overall fragility. But other threads, yet unknown to me, were waiting to be discovered.

IV

Banquets & Cameos

SUSTENANCE

Ongoing

Writing has always sustained me. I've been doing it for half my life. I lose sight of all else when I'm writing. It's a joyful release. However, I'm often also swept with guilt over the time spent lost in my world of words and pages. I worry about who and what I neglect—a chore or a friend or family member. Alan is likely the one who feels shortchanged the most.

Though he has multiple interests, Alan says he has no passion that compares to my writing. When he first said it, I felt sad for him. But the more I thought about it, the less I agreed with him—he has music and our lovable goldendoodle puppy, Winston (in honor of his hero, Winston Churchill), both of which he loves with his whole heart. I'm convinced that peace comes to Alan as well. Still, I worry.

But I can't stop writing—it is my saving grace, through which I am better able to manage all aspects of being alive. I write from depths and peaks—the hardest days and the loveliest. What sustains me on the days in between? It's worth exploring, because most days contain a few hours when I am functioning, productive, and not curled up in a ball on my bed or the couch, when the burning in my chest finally cools. When Catherine, Mom, aging, and COVID aren't first in my consciousness. What is so important that the act of writing becomes essential? And how does writing defuse the pain? Or soften it enough to permit me to focus on other, more life-sustaining activities? The act of writing shows me what I have in my life that nourishes me. This is an issue that I return to almost to the point of obsession. And I must. This is serious.

Since I tend to be depressive—a trait I believe I inherited from my mother, rooted in a childhood of shame and fear—my natural inclination is to focus on the negative. Therefore, I must consciously make space for regular assessments of what's positive. It's a worthy exercise. And an act of control that I'm capable of (we all are!).

I can't obsess about two polar opposites simultaneously, so any time spent focusing on life's bounty leaves less time for suffering over its terrors, failures, and disappointments. The most lethal of which is my attack on myself. Have I caused this crisis in my back? Am I at fault for the distance that existed between Catherine and Mom? So much of wellness has to do with my conscious awareness of my emotional and psychological processes and my willingness to monitor what triggers and quiets them. Awareness leads to balance, which is what I need in order to find peace. A hard-won balm, no question, and probably incomplete—but worth every step I take.

Today, as I sit down to write, I focus first and foremost on home. I'm thinking about the quiet peace I experience living with Alan in our smallest residence yet, our Brooklyn apartment, where we moved four years ago, downsizing from our larger apartment in New Jersey. For practicality, we are living in three rooms together, veritably insulated. It takes a strong marriage to manage such closeness, but we can claim that. We've worked for it.

Like most couples, we've had our difficulties—a few serious issues required couples therapy to detangle—but in the end, we're very good friends. We're both children of possessive mothers and passive fathers, so trust was an issue, but we've pulled through to a very safe place that buttresses me now when I'm so vulnerable following Catherine's death. Alan is my rock. And, during my stronger days, I believe I am his.

THE CROWN

1979 / Ongoing

WE ALSO HAVE OUR HOME IN EAST HAMPTON, OUR SANCTUARY and holy place, roomy enough to share with David and his miracle girls, and all of our family, friends; the place Mom and Dad visited often; the home that David grew up in; the home that Alan and I were married in and David and Marlene were married in thirty years later. Nestled in the woods, it has always been a refuge for us—the place I go to write, our oasis that Alan designed and had built while we were in the earliest stage of our relationship. There we experience concentrations of intense time together and, during down times, lots of space where we each can be alone. Outside on the property, we spend time with our extended family of towering trees, many that already watched over the property when we first moved in forty-four years ago. They are growing old with us—the fat sumptuous white pine and the black skeletal pine reminiscent of my twisted spine—living sculptures that mimic our lives together. The scrub oaks remind us of where we come from and the toll life takes, yet they have dignity too, a camaraderie and a resilience suggesting that what life takes from one, it takes from us all. We're family. All in this together. This is a home I'll never tire of. Like us, our son, grandchildren, and hopefully their children will grow old here.

Here in East Hampton, the ocean and the trees nourish me. The trees form the cocoon that shelters us. My favorite is the stately blue spruce, tall and exquisitely shaped, suggesting human sculpting. Rarely do I see such symmetry in nature. But no one and nothing altered its growth except sun, wind, rain, occasional snow, and the multicolored community of robins, goldfinch, and song sparrow birds that rush to its branches throughout the day. It stands beyond the pool, a gift to us for our wedding forty-four years ago. By now, it's easily fifty feet tall. Like us, it's showing the wear of years. Disease natural to the species has eroded its branches to a charred black.

I was devastated when I first discovered the diseased limbs. They were all I could see. Suddenly, the tree embodied all that my depression told me about aging—that once it starts, it's relentless in its rush to take over the whole body. I could no longer look at it. Eventually, I asked several arborists what could be done to save her and was told that nothing would eradicate the disease, common in recent years to the Northwest Woods where we live. No one could tell us if and how quickly the disease would take over the upper part as well. Over the past couple of years, while locked in depression, I've come close to cutting her down—so great was the pain of seeing her beautiful body diminishing. Like my own fragile body. It warned that decay and death were what waited for me. But I couldn't kill her. Nor could Alan or David. This tree is a member of our family. We decided to wait to see how she progressed over the next few seasons.

Remarkably, rather than the disease continuing to move up the tree, destroying the burst of new growth, it stopped seemingly where it was when I first discovered it. Above it, the profusion of slate blue branches, cones, and fronds continue to flourish. I named it the crown. It is its own miracle. And ours.

Sometime while writing this memoir and cataloging the gifts and losses of my life, I reversed the way I viewed the blue spruce. As was necessary in the rest of my life, I insisted that I change my focus and look at the whole tree rather than focus entirely on the wounded trunk. I found the sun still brightly painting the top branches of my beloved tree younger and younger. Despite our spruce's weakened body, at the crown, life continued excitedly. I choose that vision. Despite my vulnerable body, my aging is also marked by joys, strength, growth, discovery, imagination. These are gifts of the ground I walk on, of being alive.

REPRIEVES

2010 / 2020

Above us, the moon still lazy on its back,
the sun barely rising: my father & I,
quiet as monks, climb up the hill
to the Poor Clare Monastery.

Each move is familiar.

Like him, I bow my head,
finger rosaries in the pocket
of my overcoat, press my Missal
into the warmth under my arm.

I am preparing my soul for the Holy Sacrifice of the Mass.

THE GREATEST LOSS OF MY LIFE PRIOR TO THE DEATH OF Catherine was that of my father. He was the person in the family I was closest to. Today is the anniversary of his passing, and a great sadness hangs over me. I miss him—particularly our long talks about his early life in Ireland, what life was like when he first arrived here nine days before the Depression struck, our politics, our values. We delighted in finding new ways to make sense of the world. And we protected our friendship. Dad was a staunch Catholic and after my first marriage ended, I was known as a fallen-away Catholic. Recognizing our vulnerability, we avoided issues of Catholic orthodoxy rather than risk the conflict that might result if we pursued them. Both of us were known to lose our temper in discussions about religion, so we made a pact to avoid them. We respected that and, remarkably, remained honest with each other. Much as I hated to hurt or alienate him, I owed him the truth. Out of respect, I had to tell him that I was marrying a Jewish man, and we would be raising our child as Jewish.

His response was so loving: "I know how hard it was for you to tell me this, Honey. I love you even more that you were truthful with me. And I want you to know that I will treat David and Alan the same as I treat the rest of the grandchildren and their Catholic parents."

And he did. Apart from our religious differences, our values about most things coincided—at the forefront, our sense of justice and moral responsibility to defend the rights of all people.

The two losses, Catherine and Dad, were equally deep but unique. Catherine's death brought me face to face with a relationship that I failed at. It triggered guilt for who I wasn't and couldn't be for her. Dad's death, on the other hand, represented the loss of a deep friendship. I miss his companionship as well as his view of me, his respect despite our differences. Alongside his love was his pride. He liked me, and I liked the person I was in his eyes.

My father was closer to God than to anyone.
Kneeling beside him in the dark light
of 6 a.m. Mass, I was like him: happy,
holy, willing to give everything.

When he died, I was plagued by the image of him cold and alone in the earth. I could not fully comprehend that his soul was no longer with his body. I worried he still felt everything. That he felt abandoned. I couldn't bear his loneliness, nor mine. There was no Communion of Saints, no Heaven, no Christ waiting for him, no reunion with Mom, his brothers, sisters, and old friends. No one was waiting. It's so difficult to embrace the idea that all this heartbreak lives only in me. Dad doesn't know it. He is no more.

Yet, dare I say it? Perhaps he is. As if he hears me and feels my despair, still my good father, he offers me a dream.

Alan and I had just arrived in Ireland with our good friends, Carol and her husband, Fred, our cruising buddies. We had landed in a small fishing village on the West Coast called Kildare. It was ten years ago, a month after my father died. They both loved him, and Fred was adamant that we stop at a local pub and salute him with Guinness, Dad's favorite, and Irish coffees. The day was bright and balmy with not a hint of the rain that Ireland is known for.

The street looked like a photo in *Travel and Leisure*—cobblestone pavement, lots of storefronts offering delicious Irish bounty—scones, soda bread (though Mom's is still the best I've ever tasted), shepherd's pie, barley soup, tea, china dishware, crystal candlesticks, and, of course, traditional Aran sweaters. Even the sounds were melodic—the cowbells, the clap of boots and high heels on the cobblestones, the raspy cello voices of friends chatting, the church bells singing the hour: 3:30 p.m. All seemed to have come together to honor Dad. I was elated and tearful. How he would have loved it! How I missed him!

That night I had a dream in which he was stretched out in an open grave—no coffin, just the rich red earth as his bed. Dressed in his usual clothes—dickeys, blue and gray plaid flannel shirt buttoned at the neck as always, giving him that hint of dignity without formality, and the blue sweater Mom knit, which he wore daily around the chilly house. A prudent man, he never turned the heat above 65 degrees—warmth is what sweaters are for, he said. On his feet were the brown cashmere socks I gave him, insisting he keep his feet warm. His hands crossed on his chest. He was perfect—peaceful, unblemished, not a spot of dirt on him or his clothes. It was just as if he were napping (as he did every afternoon) peacefully in his earthen bed. The dream was simple, complete, reassuring me that he was safe, content. I had no cause for alarm. I tear with gratitude each time I revisit that dream—a message of love and renewal from that other world that threatens me: "It isn't a dark place, Honey. The light is rich and warm. Don't be afraid. I'm not," he says.

My reprieve from the ache of Catherine's loneliness—that unrelenting vision of her alone on a stretcher in a dark, painfully cold room as she waited for the fire that would consume her body—came in the form of a dream as well. I was walking alone on the beach, always a home for me and for all of us Cusack kids, raised on the Long Island Sound. I noticed that protruding from the sand were hundreds of small, gold oval frames, glinting in the sun. What the ovals contained was buried beneath the sand. I bent down, picked one frame up, and turned it over. A cameo. The image of a beautiful young woman carved out of a conch shell and framed in gold. Cath and I loved our cameos. When we were teenagers, we worked our part-time jobs to buy our favorites: cultured pearls, birthstone rings, cameos. But not for ourselves. Jewelry was to be gifted. It became our unwritten project to make sure our sister had the jewelry she craved. That tradition continued well into adulthood. I still wear those pieces. Catherine did as well.

The message of the dream was comforting. Like a signal from Catherine from wherever she was. Just as is true with Dad's death, it's my way to vacillate between no belief and the insistence that life must continue in some form or space. Catherine was the cameo. Resting safely in the sand that warmed our feet every summer day when we were kids. Perfectly preserved. And they were everywhere on the beach—telling me she's safe, warm, untainted. Pretty and without illness, enjoying this quiet return to our favorite spot. It's where she decided to rest. I took that dream as assurance from her that I could let go of that cold dark room. She is languishing peacefully in the sun. And she's everywhere—all around me. Cameos. In abundance.

Did the dream eliminate the sadness? The recrimination? No. But it eased them considerably. Those may always be with me, but so will the dream. The cameos provided an alternate scenario in which Catherine was not angry. She didn't feel abandoned. She knew—and knows now—that I love her. Such a blessing!

Where do these messages come from? I wonder. Therapist Joan responds:

> Catherine and Dad are alive deep in your unconscious, tending to you as you did them. Whatever the universe—interior or otherworldly—they are still here.

INTEGRITY & LOVE IN ABUNDANCE

1990 / 1999

THOUGH MY MOTHER'S HARSHNESS, RIGIDITY, AND JUDGMENT tainted my view of her as the caregiver of my siblings and me, she shone as a grandmother. Unlike the scolding and angry mother I knew, she was animated, youthful, and playful with her grandchildren. Who was this woman? She echoed the patient woman who designed clothes with me, all those years ago. With David, she invented new games, stretching out and playing on the floor (a maneuver she managed quite gracefully irrespective of her arthritic knees and hands). Though she claimed that she no longer had the agility to crochet or knit for us grown-up kids, suddenly her needles were clicking in perfect tempo as she created fisherman's sweaters, hats, and blankets for her six grandchildren.

Each of them was indulged by her and convinced that they were her favorite. Because she was usually alone with each of them, competitions rarely erupted. This differed sharply from her behavior with Catherine, Sonny, Jerry, and me—we had been right there, witnessing her treatment of our fellow siblings. As we grew into adulthood and moved into our own lives and homes, phone calls and visits with her shifted back and forth from warm and loving to pointed when she recounted the ways in which she was neglected or mistreated by the other three. Each of us battling to prove that we were the most reliable and she could count on us to intervene in any situation to defend her.

The competition was ongoing and relentless. Clearly, all the arrows of our attention needed to be pointed at her.

I grew tired of that dance, however, and told her I didn't want to hear her complaints about my siblings.

"Tell them about it, not me," I said countless times, both of us resentful.

She felt that I cut her off and I criticized her. But I saw through her manipulations. Hence, there were long stretches of silence between us. But with her grandchildren, she was entirely different. This is often the case with grandparents and their grandchildren. Grandparents don't raise their grandchildren, so they are not burdened with the angst parents are often subject to, and grandchildren go home.

The exception to my mother's controlling behavior was evident during my divorce and in my unmarried life that followed. She supported me during this painful time, and I was grateful. I continued to resist conversations about my siblings, and she respected that. Though she was embarrassed about my divorce, particularly due to the reactions of her sisters in Ireland and the neighbors, she disliked Tom anyway and wanted to see me happy.

We grew closer. Aware that I was stretched financially, she surprised me with the gift of a sewing machine—a top-of-the-line Singer that I'd been dreaming of. She taught me how to use it, and together we started designing and sewing clothes for me, just as we did when I was young. I was proud of the fact that I could claim "I made it myself" admitting only half the truth when friends commented on my new outfits. Mom and I were alone again, just the two of us, choosing patterns, fabrics (upholstery mostly, which offered vibrant color and texture and was quite inexpensive compared to the more traditional cotton, silk, wool). We were happy again.

Her support included my remarriage. David's birth brought us even closer—she and Dad were enthusiastic, loving, eager to babysit, and even stay for several days so that Alan and I could have an occasional vacation alone.

David's favorite game was basketball, and resourceful playmate that Mom was, she took a hefty-sized pot that served as a basket and a pair of my father's heavy woolen socks as the ball. And off they went to the living room "court." They loved playing checkers and memory too, though when she beat David at checkers, he was inconsolable. Grandmas are supposed to let you win.

But she was adamant, "Don't get sad, get mad. Then you can beat me."

I was enormously grateful that she was direct and honest with him and didn't indulge his expectation of privilege, which would only discourage him from putting forth his best effort and continue trying. Eventually he did beat her, but I'm not sure if that was a staged or authentic loss on her part. It certainly was a highlight in David's young life.

Dad too enjoyed being a grandfather and introducing David and the other grandchildren to new skills and activities. He taught David to pitch a ball. And when he was approaching ninety, he devotedly ran back and forth beside David in the scorching August sun for what seemed like hours, teaching him to ride a bike. He taught Jerry Jr., Peter, Michael, and David how to use professional tools to design their own treasures when they were each quite young. Though he wasn't a carpenter by trade, he was a gifted woodworker as evidenced by the authentic roll top desk (tongue and groove constructed) he made for Jerry, and the frames he made for Sonny's paintings.

Life was not perfect, however. When David was twelve and approaching his Bar Mitzvah, Dad told me that he could not in good conscience, as a devout Catholic, bless this conversion by attending the service. I was angry with him for taking such a narrow bigoted stance—typical of the archaic Church that I had left. Such rigidity. So unlike the father I knew. But lately, this was also him—the father I found so difficult to accept and so different from the father we grew up with. He was generally open and flexible in his thinking; this other person was difficult to love. I met this version of him so seldom that I was stunned each time I faced him—this less loving father—this narrow-minded man. This was the man that I confronted when our conversations turned to our religious differences and necessitated our pact to avoid these confrontations that could damage our relationship.

The last of these clashes was the most painful for each of us—I don't even remember what it was about—probably abortion or homosexuality (our usual battle). I was so angry, I started raising my voice, got up, and went into the house. He stayed seated on the deck. Within ten—perhaps fifteen—minutes, he got up and headed inside just as I was heading outside. We met at the door, each apologizing profusely for our anger and hurting each other, expressing our love, and promising to never allow such a painful, gratuitous battle to come between us again.

And we haven't. That pact saved us. Protected us. Allowed me to love him without reserve. But the Bar Mitzvah issue involved David and was an issue that we (I!) couldn't avoid.

Therapist Joan offers:

> Coming face to face with the differences between adult sons and daughters and their parents often precipitates battles that threaten the relationship as it did with you and your dad. We get caught up insisting that the other is wrong and we are right, and the resentment tends to seep into other more peaceful and loving aspects of the connection. Your decision and your Dad's to apologize and commit to never succumbing to the pitfalls of an argument that clearly cannot be won by either party is the most effective way I can think of to preserve the bond and continue to preserve a loving relationship.

Reluctantly I told David that his grandfather would not attend his Bar Mitzvah, and he responded, "But Grandpa isn't the one who's becoming Jewish, so why can't he come? I'm his grandson, he has to be there. I want to talk to him."

Unlike most of his friends, who relied on their parents to speak for them, David was fluent in speaking for himself, despite the fact that he later told me he thought that my silence meant I didn't care. My heart still cracks at the thought of how abandoned he must have felt. My goal had always been to encourage him to be confident in himself and his words. No voice could ever protect him as well as his own. I repeated it many times, telling him how my parents had always listened to what I had to say and the ways that that permission fortified me for my lifetime. It would strengthen him as well.

I phoned my father and told him that David wanted to speak to him.

At lunch the following Saturday, David was direct: "I'm really upset, Grandpa, that you won't be at my Bar Mitzvah. It's not fair. You and Grandma are the people closest to me next to my mom and dad. This is an important occasion for me. You should share that day with me like you do when you come to my violin concerts. And I guess if you don't come, Grandma won't either."

My mother rushed to clarify that she would be there with or without my father.

"And I will be there too, David," my father followed up. "When your Mom told me you wanted to talk to me, I knew what it was about. So, I spoke to that young priest who just joined our congregation and told him about my struggle. He understood and said that there would be nothing wrong with me attending your Bar Mitzvah. In no way did it reflect on my loyalty to the Church."

"WOW! GRANDPA! That's awesome!" David was thrilled, grateful.

Mom and I were tearful, silent. It was a stunning moment in the history of our family. A victory for love, for David's ability to speak up about what was most important to him, and for Dad's pursuit of a more flexible, modern priest who assured him that his attendance at his grandson's Bar Mitzvah in no way disrespected or compromised his commitment to the Church. Integrity and love in abundance from my son and my father. My mother and I so grateful, so blessed.

TRANSFIXED

2015 / 2017

FAST FORWARD TWENTY-FIVE YEARS TO MY OWN TURN AS A grandparent. The arrival of Cassidy Vaughn Handler, David's first child, was imminent. I was thrilled that her middle name, Vaughn, was chosen to honor me. Vaughn and Siobhan, the Irish name for Joan, may not be spelled alike, but their sound is almost identical, soaring, bird-like, free. When David placed tiny Cassidy in my arms, I was transfixed. For the second time in my life—the first being when I held him after he slipped out of me and into the world—I was instantly, sublimely in love. Cradling my granddaughter, the universe shifted.

Like the renewal of faith that overtook me during urgent life circumstances, restoring a seemingly uninterrupted dialogue with God, I was also returned to the scene of my son's birth through the miracle of this child, my infant son's twin! Their similarities were and continue to be uncanny—tender, musical, smart, with a delicious sense of humor, love of language, abundant blonde silky curls, and pink porcelain skin. Two philosophers from day one. Her likeness to me as well as her father was obvious to everyone. Beyond her green eyes, she has many of my same passions. How do we know where preferences originate? Nature or nurture? Eight years later, her love of design, the antique objects she gravitates toward, and of course, her love of beautiful clothes, and books—reading them, telling stories, writing her own. All loves of mine. And here she is—at the center of my life. My senior life.

A second child, Elodie Rush Handler, entered the world three years after Cassidy. Once again, the universe shifted. The magic intensified exponentially. Another brilliant creation! How utterly herself she was from her first moments in the world. An old soul, with clear likes and dislikes as if she'd been here for a long time, long enough to have sifted through life's possibilities and make her choices. No one could try to change this girl's diaper or feed her when she wasn't ready without triggering bellowing that rivaled that of a banshee.

There's nothing shy or understated about her. She loves what she loves (like music and dance) to the point of gleeful laughing from her earliest days. Compelled to vibrate and bounce in her high chair or on the floor in her own rhythmic dance. What she feels takes over her face. She's smart, very smart, and intuitive—knows her power and uses it—recognizing my vulnerabilities, teasing me, and exercising her right to say "no!" Spunky, adamant, and as independent and confident in her own right to be as her older sister. So far from the child I was.

Intimidated by Elodie at first, I wanted her to like me, but she dismissed any cajoling or persuasion on my part. She decided in her time and on her own terms who she invited in. And it took a while. I was unsure and shy—I had to earn this child's trust. But by and by, she let me in. Mostly because I didn't rush her. I waited until she was ready, and she decided that she was interested in me. Then we became friends. We adore each other. I revel in the beauty of who she is and our differences.

The hardest part of mothering for me was letting David go as he drifted gracefully from one phase of development to the next. Each progression brought loss as well as celebration. The price I had to pay as Mom was relinquishing the baby or toddler he'd been to this new stage—be it crawling, walking, surrendering his bottle, diapers, making words—and more words, then sentences—as he grew into himself.

And here I am again, reliving those days with the beautiful children who came from him.

How I envy the children for their groundedness, their self-assurance, their joy! Watching them now, I return to the one photo I have of the mad, sad little girl I was with the long fat curls who didn't want her picture taken. So much more than anger reflected there. Who was this child? A child of four, so old, so brittle that nothing could soften that small face. Seventy-five years later, Cassidy and Elodie are reincarnations without the trauma and sadness. Like the child I might have been.

THEN THE POEMS CAME

2005

My mother died several years before Catherine and my father, after suffering through a prolonged battle with pancreatic cancer. Though I missed her once she was gone, I also felt a quiet relief. She had spent three months in palliative care at Calvary Hospital where she was impeccably and lovingly cared for by the staff and doctors. Surrounded by all of us (except Sonny—steadfast that he would not visit her or attend her funeral), the familiar anger, recriminations, resentments between all of us disappeared. She was a remarkably changed person when she got sick—the comments tainted with innuendo disappeared, her pitting my siblings and me against each other stopped. In their place was her recognition and appreciation of each one of us—Jerry, Catherine, me, and Dad, all her grandchildren.

She became easy to love. The generosity she had demonstrated in my early years and later with her grandchildren was revived and she was full of love and gratitude. She knew she was dying, and she was at peace. She finally understood that she was loved. Remarkably, she seemed happy. Though we never talked about it, I imagine she was looking forward to what she believed would be a reunion with her beloved mother. My heart breaks to think that what waited for her, for Dad, and for Catherine was darkness, nothingness.

Those days, my mother and I were happy together. She was once again my champion. And I hers. She encouraged my writing, read many of my poems. I brought her books to read.

"Joan, write *your* life! You tell the truth!" she encouraged after having read *Angela's Ashes,* Frank McCourt's account of his early life and his mother's reportedly promiscuous affairs. "He's just saying that to sell books! No mother would do that in front of her children!" she exclaimed, irate.

I told her I was writing my story and read to her from the coming-of-age memoir I was working on—*Confessions of Joan the Tall.* "It's all in there, Mom," I told her, referring somewhat obliquely to what I chose not to read.

She responded, "Including me in all my glory. Even the bitch I sometimes was." She giggled. She was not a woman who ever used profanity, and she lowered her voice when she said what she viewed as a curse. We laughed at the truth of that comment. Such transparency. Such permission. Such psychological distance she'd traveled. My mother said it was okay to tell the truth—about all of it, including her. My loving mother was back.

When she died, I was left with the mother who unabashedly loved me. The irony stuns me. I had lived by Mom's commandment: never speak outside of anything that goes on inside our four walls. And I didn't. To my knowledge, none of us did. Not to each other, not to friends. But on her deathbed, she gave me permission to speak the truth. New poems came, and I confided in them.

FINDING BALANCE

2020

It's May, six months from when Catherine passed away. My spirit seems to have lightened, but I am ashamed that this is happening in the center of grief. It's a new guilt. One that threatens to take over. I can't think of a time in my life when guilt didn't torture me. It's always there, ready to lunge. So dark, so penetrating. So Catholic.

Therapist Joan speaks:

> One of the most difficult feelings to accept in the loss of a loved one is the relief that comes with their passing.

"How can I feel relieved? I loved Catherine," I respond.

Therapist Joan reflects:

> How can you not? Whole segments of your psyche are freed from the clutter—often torment—of worry, increased burden, decreased time for yourself, the loneliness that accompanies being a caregiver to another, particularly an ill loved one. Suddenly your time and energies are freed from the weight of carrying her. She is no longer in pain—physical or emotional. That ache is gone, albeit replaced by grief. Catherine held on as long as she could until her body finally gave up. It couldn't fight

anymore. It no longer had the strength it took to call forth breath. The pain that has been part of your everyday experience with Catherine during her last three months (and so many times before), is gone. That part of your life is over. The sister you tried to care for is no more.

It was true, though I still felt ashamed that I felt so much brighter after Catherine's death. Now there was room in my life for Alan, my granddaughters, David, and my girlfriends. Following my therapeutic instructions to myself, I repeated this over and over when guilt threatened to crush me. And it helped.

Though I continue to obsess on how inadequate a sister I was and how distant, fortunately I'm very slowly beginning to forgive myself for the fissure that existed between us. I remind myself that months ago, David and Alan helped me to see that I was not responsible for changing Catherine. I needed to accept that fact. It was what made our last visits fun and tender. There's a purity in my love for her now. Her smiling face pops up everywhere, greeting me, "Hi Honey!" After almost seventy-nine years, I have a sister!

NESTING

2020

THE PEACE I'M ENJOYING LATELY OPENS TIME AND ENERGY FOR ME, allowing me to focus on my marriage and the movement of my life. Alan and I are graceful partners at this point in our lives. It is one of the advantages of aging and a well-seasoned marriage. Most of the adjustments are peaceful. We seldom fight. We've been there, done that. Disagreements that once resulted in battles have softened into reasoned negotiations (for the most part!). There are still a few surprises. We know each other.

All my life I've avoided the middle—
the watered-down version, all
colors muted—middle of the road,
midlife, even middle of my body.
But here at the center of this marriage,
it's that place between us where
truth sits: the third party in the room
that hears him & hears me.

Though outside, COVID-19 continues to roar. Tucked here in our cozy apartment, I have no sense of that fear and despair, provided I don't turn on the TV. And I don't. Except *for Law and Order: Special Victims Unit* in the evening. And the 6:30 news (alas, I'm addicted). Alan and I are enjoying a quiet grace. I write or read, and lately he reads as well. He was never before a reader, save for psychology books and *Time* magazine.

(I'm convinced that PhD training ruins pleasure reading for many. It did for me for several years.) Alan has turned a corner, galloping through book after book—mostly political nonfiction and history. His current favorite is a biography of Churchill. I still haven't gotten used to it. It gives me such a giggle to look up and see him engrossed in a book instead of Scrabble, chess, sudoku, or watching tennis on TV.

Before we moved to Brooklyn, we lived in a large, three-bedroom apartment in Fort Lee, New Jersey, so it became natural for us to choose our own spaces in separate rooms. Though luxurious on the one hand, so much territory was also distancing—each of us going off to our private corners and coming together only for meals and bed. Not so in Brooklyn. First, the rooms are smaller and fewer than outside of the city. It's a two-bedroom—one for us and one for Alan's keyboard and Cassidy and Elodie's sleepovers. May the days be few until we can resume those sweet visits. We love them so! The result of this blueprint is that we have no room for a separate office or study. The open living room serves as kitchen, dining area, offices, and living space, and lately, a play area for Winston. Alan and I enjoy our two oversized easy chairs that are trim but ungainly nonetheless, particularly to the designer in me. Alan and I laugh about the fact that comfort is his prime mover and design is mine. He wins on this one, hands down.

This middle collects all the gestures:
the words & not-words. Perhaps we
can live here, lie down, roll into her
safe arms—she has room for the two of us.

Here, I sometimes feel like I'm living in a European town. When I lived in Fort Lee, it was predominantly White, Asian, and straight. Williamsburg is every color of the rainbow, every age, every sexual orientation. I love it! It's also reminiscent of our beloved cruise vacations—high above the Hudson and far from civilization on the streets below, our focus on just the two of us. We do everything in this room—read, talk on the phone, pay bills, listen to music, watch TV, stare at One World Trade Center (formerly known as the Freedom Tower) and the Empire State Building outside our windows. I even write in the center of this busy little space. And during quarantine, we talk more than we did in our spacious Fort Lee apartment. About everything (well, almost everything) that wanders through our minds. David and our granddaughters, Catherine, COVID, what Carol had to say when she called earlier, and on, and on, and on.

Each of us is responsible for small chores in the house—the rest we leave for another day. There's always another day. Alan puts on his mask and shops for food. I tend to the laundry and dishes. We both cook, though since he's had his air fryer, he does most of it. He reads recipes and makes his own garlic butter. I make wild rice—enough for the coming weeks. He chops onions. I caramelize them. He vacuums. I Windex the dining-room table and sanitize the kitchen counters. We read, watch movies, TV series, MSNBC, CNN, FaceTime with David, Cassidy, and Elodie.

Shameless, Alan is the comic, offering up his pride to ridiculousness whenever he can. Witness my wide-brimmed turquoise sun hat perched on the top of his abundant platinum (once mahogany) curls as he waltzes, not quite gracefully, to some favorite show tune. "Gigi," "I Feel Pretty," "Why Can't a Woman Be More Like a Man" for the screams and giggles of Elodie and Cassidy on FaceTime. Or the twisted faces and body contortions he often makes to engage or appease them. Or his shout-out to me in his booming bass voice, "How now, brown cow!" "There, there, big bear!" when I'm deep into writing.

Winston, Alan's latest contribution to the family entertainment, keeps us on high alert with his antics.

She holds our places, lets
his shade & mine mingle
together without giving in
completely.

This closeness might seem claustrophobic to many, but we're happy here. Friends wonder if we feel cramped or tired of each other, but we don't. The floor-to-ceiling windows looking out on the East River and the Manhattan skyline seem to stretch the space. To guarantee fun and fantasy and lift our mood when it threatens to topple, after dinner, it's our way to watch our favorite musical from the fifties and sixties. Last night, *South Pacific*. The night before, *Oklahoma*. Last week, *Gigi, Funny Face, Camelot,* and another I can't recall. Tonight, maybe *The Sound of Music, Fiddler,* or *My Fair Lady,* our favorite. Side by side in bed, we sing along, waving our arms in time with the music. We're young! Very young!

What safer place than this—
where each of us gets & gives:
no side left unattended in the
lap of Good Mother we rush to.

WHEN DOES THE GRATITUDE START?

2021

Though I try my best not to look at media coverage of the pandemic, I feel compelled to check in daily for the latest update, usually on the 6:30 news. I keep waiting to hear that the number of people taken by the disease is diminishing—I imagine that would go a long way in easing my depression, but that doesn't happen. Hope diminishes. The numbers just multiply exponentially along with the sirens shrieking, the towers of white body bags that wait in makeshift containers to be buried. Our one happy moment each evening is still Manhattan's rituals of clapping, banging pots and pans in appreciation of our health care workers, who relentlessly day after day turn themselves inside out to save the dying. In the terror that hovers over each of us in the midst of a pandemic, my one relief is that I'm able to still be medicated. I am taking the same antidepressant medication, the same prescription, and the same dose as I did before this depression hit. The one change is that my psychopharmacologist has added an additional medication that is known to augment my previous dosage. I continue to notice that my depression is lifting. A touch of hope. May both continue.

Periodically, I catch myself checking my left hand—it's a ridiculous habit I have—reassuring myself that the long lifeline that stretches across my hand to the other side, circling almost to the front is, in fact, a predictor of a long life. Not always, but most days. Is this how far

Dad's reached? He lived to ninety-nine-and-a-half. I wish I'd checked Mom's. She made it to eighty-eight. If I knew her lifeline, I could almost predict my future—be grateful for my extra years. Get to the place in an aging (disappearing!) life where gratitude replaces fear and dread of the end, the extra days, months, years you've been given over what's expected, like the lift and bravado in the poet Donald Hall's voice, when he announced that death was nowhere to be seen. I want to get to that place, but I don't trust myself—I don't think I'll be able to be grateful for my age until well after ninety, closer to ninety-five. As greedy as I am, always wanting more than my share. Still, it would be so nice to celebrate each birthday with joy that you're marking another year—how fortunate, how gifted—so much better than this lonely place where I'm facing eighty in a few months and dreading it.

When does the gratitude start? I want it to start. I want to not be scared. To be glad to face each new year knowing how lucky I am to be here.

But how long I'll live is only half the puzzle. Next, I study my talent line. Always a tricky subject. I can't be sure which line it is. The one I think delights me in its long stretch almost to my wrist—certainly to the bone at the base of my thumb—reassuring me that when I doubt my writing gifts (as I'm prone to more often than I'd like), the map of my palm insists that I'm wrong. The curved road stretching down my hand is anything but short. But what if that's not the talent line? What if it's the line that's next to it? I do what I can to halt these obsessive thoughts by refusing to indulge them any further—but not until I end up where I started. Concluding that the news isn't good.

Or maybe it is.

ANOTHER GOOD MOTHER

1975–2005 / 2020

WHAT WOKE ME EARLY THIS MORNING WAS ANOTHER DREAM—this one about my former psychotherapist, Henny Glatzer, PhD. Not surprisingly, I don't remember the details. More important was how I felt when I awoke. I felt like the woman she knew. Like the woman she respected and valued. An awakening: I am loved. Despite her death several years ago, my unconscious has kept Henny alive and present. I need to remind myself what this means. My dreams are telling me I can trust myself.

Meticulously professional, Henny broke no rules. She didn't tell me she loved and valued me. Her manner told me. My sense of self gradually lightened in her presence from depression and self-criticism to liking. She encouraged every independent impulse, took me very seriously, even laughed at my jokes. I remember a day in group therapy when a woman reproached me for not paying more attention to my weight; another said I was too interested in clothes. When I raised these in my private session, Henny dismissed the woman's comments, chiding me (albeit gently) for my willingness to accept as truth every criticism leveled at me.

"There's nothing wrong with your weight. And what's wrong with loving clothes?" she stated plainly.

Henny was my Good Mother. She believed in me. Encouraged me to see myself through a different lens than that of my own mother (loving at times, but also angry and possessive), the nuns, the boys in the alley, Sonny ready to lunge, my mother-in-law's rejection because I wasn't Jewish. The list of my critics was endless. Henny helped me to turn out the lights in those cold rooms. The dream said I have much to say about the people who molded me. So much gratitude! Who and what haven't I focused on? My mother? Her sweet and generous side. My angel granddaughters, Cassidy and Elodie. Joys! This is how I choose to spend my days. And hopefully starve this depression.

It also told me how deeply I was—and am—loved. That awareness lives inside me now. I can trust it. A woman, a mother figure whom I respected and whose intelligence was widely acclaimed, believed in me. Though I haven't thought about her in many months, she arrives when I am most vulnerable. Most troubled about my ability to care for myself. At times when I most need to go back into therapy.

I need someone to talk to. I don't want to do this alone. I don't have to, the dream tells me. Henny still hears me. I can call on her whenever I need. You, reader, can hear me. Even when the reader is myself, reflecting on what I've written. These are the times when I most need to write. I feel enriched when I write. Enriched when I think of Henny. Writing is healing, as is Henny.

ORCHIDS IN TALL VASES

2020

MOTHER'S DAY WEEKEND, 2020. WRITTEN ALL OVER THE FACES of Cassidy and Elodie is unbridled joy in seeing us. David, Marlene, and the girls have returned from their two months quarantine at Marlene's mom's home in Florida and settled in our home in East Hampton, and Alan and I drove out to be with them. All of us, giggling and dancing like puppies. Such rapture hugging my son! The celebratory infusion after two months with no contact. As safe as we can manage forbidden hugs, the four adults. With the girls, we give only "leg hugs." No kisses of course.

On the carved teak trunk that abuts the couch, Cassidy's welcome display—a rainbow she drew and painted, a framed photo of me, a heart-shaped photo of her as a newborn, a second painting covered with bright red hearts, small luminous shells and a conch she'd collected on any one of many trips to the beach, and a larger shell she'd painted in bright happy colors.

Grilled cheese sandwiches and tomato soup for lunch, then the afternoon on the red couch in front of the fire. The girls down for a nap. Within minutes, Cassidy is back. Nap abandoned, she's been dreaming of us playing Dress Up, our favorite game and the perfect choice while Elodie naps. It is time to prepare the kingdom. Toys removed from the parade route. Next, our outfits! Donning long dresses—me in the pink one I wore to David and Marlene's wedding and she, digging through her collection, decides on the pink one, so we match.

"Today we'll both be queens!" she proclaims. Usually she's the queen and I'm the princess, but she is extra generous after such a long separation.

Once dressed, she looks at my sneakers. "Oh, Grandma, you have to take off those shoes! Queens don't wear shoes!"

But I prevail, reminding her how prone Grandma is to falling. She accepts that gracefully, combs my hair and hers, hands me my wand, and we march through our kingdom, two beaming, elegant queens! Along the parade route, our subjects—Mommy, Daddy, and Pop-Pop. Dinner is lovely, intimate. Once the girls are asleep for the night, the four of us enjoy some quiet time together. Catherine, the center of this banquet. We can finally love and grieve her together as we haven't been able to in quarantine. I give Marlene the cashmere shawl I'd been holding for Catherine but wasn't able to give her. They had a warm and loving connection. In one of her hallucinatory travels, Catherine told us that Marlene had come to the hospital several times to visit, and she'd brought the girls.

"Are they beautiful!" Catherine exclaimed. "What a great mother. I don't know how she does it."

In real life, always concerned that Catherine had company, Marlene contacted several occupational and physical therapy friends who either worked at the hospital where Catherine was or had friends who did and asked them to visit her as often as possible. Several did. They loved and laughed with her.

This morning, there are more Happy Mother's Day cards from the girls, orchids in tall vases for both moms from David, of course, a sumptuous brunch feast of French toast, raspberries, and whipped cream. Then a movie, *Beauty and the Beast,* with my Cassidy beside me, Elodie on Pop-Pop's lap or playing ball when she grows tired of sitting still. Like him, Elodie prefers moving over sitting. She's a wanderer.

After naptime, we congregate with crackers and a cluster of cheeses with wine and apple juice on the deck. Though the sun is high, the wind calls for shawls or jackets, so we all sit around wrapped in our respective toasty cocoons. Eating. Laughing. Joyful! Then a bath in the big tub for the girls with Grandma in attendance. Dinner. Sumptuous! Takeout from our favorite restaurant in Sag Harbor. Garlic knots and the many faces of pastas: lasagna, carbonara, bolognese, white clam sauce! Bedtime ritual for the girls with Mommy and Daddy. Grandma and Pop-Pop curled by the fire. Suddenly asleep.

How impossible it is to feel old and depressed when I'm in the company of my grand girls.

Monday morning, the girls feast on Cheerios with Pop-Pop while I giggle my way through my fake cappuccino before heading to the car for our trip back to Brooklyn. At the door the girls, their parents, and we vigorously wave, no kisses of course, call, "Love you, Grandma! Love you, Pop-Pop!"

All of us blowing kisses! Blowing kisses! And "Thank you. So wonderful. Drive safely. Love you! Love you too!"

IT'S STILL NOT SAFE TO RETURN TO BROOKLYN

2020

A SUNNY, JUNE DAY OUTSIDE MY WINDOW, BUT IT REMAINS GRAY inside. It's June 3, what would have been Catherine's eighty-second birthday. I pull myself out of bed and go to the kitchen to have breakfast with Cass and El. I'll resist my inclination to go back to bed. Usually, a place of solace and quiet but today, one of sadness. I don't need to be alone today. It won't bring Catherine back. Loss is not all there is.

I need to keep reminding myself of what I have in my life. Today and every day. This is how I teach myself how to be old.

I'm writing! I dreamt of Henny! Making sausage and peppers with David for tonight's dinner. The lush and tender nest that is my marriage to Alan, who knows my heart better than any other, who, besides Henny, truly is my Good Mother. The amazing David, our son, generous, wise, and very funny, unafraid to be openly loving or confrontational, depending on the moment or need. Meticulous, playful dad. He and Alan enjoying sparring at tennis. Cassidy and Elodie making cards covered with hearts, spinning their scooters around the tennis court. The sun outside my window painting the dogwood leaves a bright lime, in places close to lemon. I'm a redhead again, thanks to Marlene—my two inches of steel gray roots camouflaged behind a vibrant cap of maple—the color of David's violin. More heart cards from Elodie and

Cassidy. I am loved. I am not alone. This banquet is what's teaching me what it is to be old. How to reduce the depression.

My heavy heart today is not only centered on Catherine. Alan and I are in East Hampton where we come to be with David and his family for long weekends. It's Wednesday, and we stayed longer than expected because of the violence exploding around the country after George Floyd's killing at the hands of a Minneapolis policeman. NYC, particularly our home borough of Brooklyn, is on lockdown and enforced curfew with many streets impassable. Peaceful (for the most part) demonstrations all over the country protest this travesty, but sadly, hatemongers from the extreme left and right as well as Machiavellian types who commandeer the marches and turn them into violent displays of hatred and destruction have left us all reeling. The cause is protest against the inhuman treatment of the Black community. Most of the protesters are committed to just that—peaceful expressions of dissent against a brutal and inhuman act. Not an act. A series of acts. Change must come for us to continue to exist in this world with any measure of dignity. Our country overwhelmingly supports the need for this bigotry to end and for peace to exist among all our citizens. The responsibility for waging that battle and keeping it in the forefront of our consciousness for the rest of our days lies with each of us. It's our destiny. We're ready, but, alas, it's still not safe to return to Brooklyn.

Cassidy just came in and brought me my turquoise straw hat and a peach scarf to wrap around it, and now I'm wearing it as is her wish. Collision of joy and loss. Keep my eyes on these children and on the swells of people who band together to repair the damage done to their cities by the violence. The lawnmower is singing outside—always a bright sound of summer for me, but today there's a darkness to it, a grief. And yes, it's Catherine's birthday.

Because Michael went home on weekends, Cath was alone for many birthdays, so Alan and I would pick her up and take her out for dinner. I remember her eightieth, in particular. It had been my hope to arrange a party for her as I had for her seventieth, but Alan and I were in the throes of moving three homes into two and all the craziness that goes with that. I was exhausted. I couldn't plan a party. I had no room in my life to do anything except obsess over what treasures to take to which home. Brooklyn? East Hampton? The one-bedroom apartment in Fort Lee that serves as the CavanKerry Press office?

Suffice it to say that the only way we could celebrate Cath on her eightieth was to stick to our usual routine and take her to dinner in the neighborhood. She was delighted as was I and picked a favorite restaurant where the five of us—she, our brother Jerry, Dad, Alan, and I—had years ago gone monthly to enjoy some family time. Alas, the restaurant was closed—they'd gone out of business, news of which left us a bit squeamish and sad. But undaunted, we set out to find another. Close by, there was a large sign several stories above the street announcing in rainbow colors the opening of a new restaurant that seemed perfect. We decided to try it. We walked in the door and were greeted by a rather shabby wooden staircase that extended three floors up. This wouldn't work. Neither Cath nor I could climb that many stairs without having trouble breathing. Just as we were about to leave, a gentleman came into the small foyer and said, "We have a lift that will take you up!" We laughed at the prospect of being carried by what looked like a forklift and decided to give it a try. Cath first, then me. Alan mounted the stairs on his own. The experience was hilarious, and we arrived upstairs at the restaurant in good spirits ready for a lovely birthday dinner.

What greeted us was a page torn out of a beach life throwaway—round plastic tables and chairs. No tablecloths, of course. Paper plates and plastic knives and forks. No menu. A few items scribbled on a blackboard—pizza, hot dogs and burgers, Coke, beer. Some boxes of supplies along the walls. A few raucous drinkers downing beer. A far cry from the elegant dinner we'd imagined. Stunned at the ridiculousness of the scene, the three of us just laughed and laughed, had pizza, and laughed some more. The scene stayed with me all day and well into the evening. How often Catherine and I laughed about it over the last two years. It was a night we treasured.

The morning after her eighty-second, I wake with a hole in my chest. I stay in bed all day. Grief is and must be reckoned with. A happy memory insulated me yesterday. Today my heart burns.

V

Keep Them Close

PRIVILEGED

Ongoing

REFLECTING ON THE PRIVILEGES OF MY LIFE RETURNS ME TO MY early years as an evolving child and young adult, and I am struck by the opportunities that my siblings and I were blessed with. While we were a typical Edgewater family in that we had limited financial resources, our parents, particularly Mom, were committed to providing us with more advantages than we could afford on Dad's salary as a plumber—parochial school from grade school through college, art lessons for Sonny, piano for Catherine and me. Our mother made it possible. Uneducated beyond grade school but smart and very resourceful, she applied to Catholic Charities for a job as a home case worker when Catherine started high school. Generally speaking, women in her generation didn't work outside of the home. In fact, she was the only mother I knew who did. Like her, the women in the neighborhood where I grew up were housewives married to Irish and German tradesman—electricians, carpenters, and plumbers—tending to as many children as the Lord decided they should have. Caring for their family was a full-time job and their primary responsibility. But my mother decided that once we were all in school and Catherine reached eighth grade, Catherine could take care of us and I would cook dinner, so Mom could go to work and start saving for our college tuition. College loans for students didn't exist then. But that would not have been a question for Mom. Committed to exposing us to the best that life had to offer, she was clear that we had to attend a Catholic college, and she had to make that possible. So, she did.

I don't think I ever thought of my mother as having sacrificed for us. I wish I had thanked her. This is the type of realization that advancing age allows. My inclination in the past has been to chastise myself for not starting this process when my mother was alive, but I'm changing. I'm who I am, and as long as I'm doing my best, I'm doing great. Or close to it. It's that acceptance of myself that makes it possible to have these memories. In the past, I would have repressed them (and did) because they triggered guilt and pain. Without the compulsion to criticize myself for not being the stand-up perfect person I felt I should be, many of my memories remained hidden. And my anger with my mother prevented me from knowing her graces. Many hurts came between us, but in focusing on them over the years, I neglected acknowledging the Mom who stitched my petticoat and bought me silver shoes. There are other facets of her that I am gradually recognizing. The process of writing this book makes it possible for me to do that.

A friend once observed, "Your mother taught you what to expect from a friend."

Something I've never thought about! And it is true. She taught me to fight and to know what real mothering looked like. In that image of us working together on my white peau de soie dress, we were very best friends. I'm humbled by all the ways that my aging and this process of conscious remembering have given my mother back to me. I have allowed myself to love her all over again.

This memory of my mother also triggers my sadness for her. She always seemed so unhappy. I thought she regretted her life, but the more I watch her now from the perspective of a long life lived, I'm not so sure that she was unhappy. Though she might not admit it, I think she enjoyed her household duties. Though she was no fan of housework, she seemed to love cooking and baking for us. I remember coming home from school with Marie to a delicious large chocolate chip cake waiting for us. Marie and I were thrilled, poured some milk, and settled down to this wonderful surprise. Dad's favorite cake was pineapple upside down cake, and she made these often as well.

Her favorite activity though was working in the yard. She loved flowers, from the hollyhocks that grew to the height of the house to the geraniums that lined the stoop steps. There were yellow and red roses of every shade wherever she could find space among the pansies, petunias, and fresh mint that took over the front of the house. The backyard was a celebration of tomatoes—plump, bright red, and juicy. It was such fun going out with her in the morning before school to pick a bouquet for Catherine, Jerry, and me to take to our respective Sisters who taught us. (Sonny said he was too old to bring flowers to a teacher, so he wasn't interested.)

Besides gardening she loved knitting sweaters—authentic Aran patterns—for each of us and crocheting doilies for the living room chairs. She proudly announced that her father taught her to knit and crochet. If she didn't like some aspect of the house, she would change it. From painting the walls, to hanging wallpaper, to sawing a bureau in two to make night tables for Catherine and me. Everything she did demonstrated how proficient a homemaker she was. Every week she made a trip to Hearn's basement, her favorite department store over an hour away, to search for homeware galore: china cups, a kettle, fabric for clothes for Catherine and me, kitchen curtains, a pressure cooker, a small statue or trinket that caught her eye. Those were her special days when she let the house take care of itself and treated herself to a shopping hunt. It may well have been her favorite activity. She rarely missed a week.

Looking back now and picturing her with her flowers, tools, knitting needles, and trinkets, I picture her satisfied, even happy, having spent long days doing things she loved to do, things that she did by herself that went far beyond her domestic duties as wife and mother. Perhaps her moodiness was only in our company—four kids born over six years requiring constant supervision and care with a husband who never punished us. The more I think of it, I picture her smiling as she picked her tomatoes, even lightly singing her favorite song, "Too-Ra-Loo-Ra-Loo-Ral . . ." So many happy memories. Such love comes with them. I feel happy thinking of my mother as the free spirit I'm finally meeting.

My privilege continues. With my education, I warranted good professional jobs with good salaries. I have a healthy loving family. I'm married to another psychologist. We're blessed with a loving son, two granddaughters, two homes, and financial security. I'm White. I am privileged.

I'm pain-free.

But I'm a woman too. For many men and women, physical size is an important determinant of intellectual ability. Small is often seen as fragile, needing to be taken care of, not as smart as a man. Here my height has served me well. During the countless years that women were dismissed and relegated to lesser responsibilities and positions, I honestly had no sense of bias against me as a woman. Or of men treating me as inferior. Tall is smart. Tall is stately. Tall is strong. While I mourned my imposing size for so many years, my height opened doors for me. Men, I've always suspected, avoid confrontation with a tall woman because they aren't sure of our strength—how physically capable we are. Looking eye to eye with a man brought me respect, a rare experience for women until recently. Men treated me as if I might well be as smart and strong as they were. Tall doesn't always fall. Sometimes she prevails.

BACK TO SQUARE ONE

2020

IT'S HELPFUL FOR ME TO SPOTLIGHT POSITIVE MOMENTS IN MY LIFE, to offset the challenges of my body, which have accompanied me through the pandemic. As aging becomes increasingly apparent, I am forced to circle back to my spine. I've always been terrorized by the thought of debilitating pain returning. The fact that it erupted again following my third and last fall triggered panic. My focus had been on the fractured foot and sacrum—both of which were healing well according to Dr. O'Leary and my ankle doctor, so neither addressed this new discomfort. A full body x-ray and CT scan were needed. Dr. O'Leary and I scheduled another appointment and reviewed the results together in a small dark room that reminded me of a cell. I was trembling. Dr. O'Leary felt frighteningly close to me. Unfortunately, Alan couldn't join us. That left me more anxious and tentative than if he'd been there.

When I saw the films, I was devastated—the deterioration in my cervical and thoracic vertebrae was considerable. Terrifying. What I saw was a crumbling ladder of fraying bones. In various states of dissolution. They appeared like the statues I'd seen at ruins in Pompeii. When would they all break off and topple? How much time did the scaffolding of my body have? Any one of several discs could account for the resurgence of pain. But nothing could be concluded. How was this spine capable of keeping me erect? A blazing heat flew from my belly into my head, and I kept losing focus. Almost passing out. Meanwhile, Dr. O'Leary tried to reassure me that an extension of the current fusion was unnecessary now. But should I want to initiate a consultation, he also offered me referrals to colleagues who were specialists in osteotomy (which he was not), the surgery that might eventually be called for, which involved breaking the current fusion and creating a new, more extensive one. I declined the referrals. My heart was banging in my chest. I told him I couldn't imagine another surgery.

I saw the concern in Dr. O'Leary's face. It mirrored mine. Within days, I had no memory of having seen him or the films, and I focused on the unexplained pain as the only complication of that fall. Paralyzed emotionally, I knew there was nothing to do but wait and see if the pain subsided. For one who is so short on patience, the wait was interminable.

I had one hope. It occurred to me that before my fusion I had always felt back pain when I was in a draft of any kind—air conditioning or an open window. I prayed (this was one of those times that faith returned instantaneously) that the current pain was due to a different ventilation system in our new Brooklyn apartment. Perhaps a draft was causing the pain. I tried several new sleeping positions over the next days and weeks, and gradually, miraculously, the pain started to lessen until it disappeared completely. I was elated!

I called Dr. O'Leary and told him I was feeling better. He expressed his relief, and we made an appointment for May when, unfortunately, COVID was still making our decisions for us. From the way the virus was controlled in New York, I was sure I'd be able to see him sometime in August or September. Fortunately, I received the vaccine, so I was hopeful that I would be able to be examined in person once I've got my second dose. A virtual visit would not do. He needed to physically assess my status. But I was optimistic and thankfully the pain was gone.

BUT EVERYTHING MOVED SLOWLY, AND I PUT OFF MAKING AN APPOINTMENT. Though I liked Dr. O'Leary very much and associated him with empathy, kindness, and extensive knowledge about my back history, I rationalized that there was nothing new he could tell me. I hadn't had any falls since I last saw him, and I assumed nothing had changed since I was not in pain. We had agreed that I'd see him annually—but it was now almost two years since my last visit. So, believing my spine was stable, I relaxed. Until late one night I was lying in bed on the edge of sleep and suddenly, the images of those devastating scans jolted me awake.

How could I have forgotten them? Oh my God! Seeing them for the first time had been the most devastating experience since my initial diagnosis and recommendation of fusion. When I looked at the crumbling vertebrae, I couldn't imagine how my fragile spine was sturdy enough to hold and move my body. My head began to spin. I was my spine's protector, and I had neglected her. Fire rushed into my face. I spent days trying to soothe myself by emphasizing the fact that I'd changed my ways in the last year and continued to do my daily walks as we had agreed I needed to.

But now I had to call him and make an appointment. I needed to know if my back was holding its own. Or had the deterioration continued? Was there a day in the future when my spine would collapse? When would I again face that terrible choice—osteotomy or wheelchair? *Please Lord, don't let him tell me I need another fusion,* I prayed. *I'm sorry for only coming to you in an emergency.*

So, I finally called Dr. O'Leary, and his first available appointment was in two weeks. That seemed like forever.

"Nothing's available sooner?" I asked.

"I'm afraid not," his receptionist answered. "Besides, we need that time to schedule the CT scan and full body x-ray."

"I did them last time!" I replied.

"Dr. O'Leary has ordered them again."

Oh God! What will they reveal this time?

SILENCE

2021

SUNDAY NIGHT, 4 A.M. AWAKE. THE MOON IS HIGH AND FULL, spreading more light than usual in the room. A welcome, of sorts. Remnants of a dream returns. This time, I talk to myself—at first with a hint of accusation:

"Why don't you let people love you?" Thereafter, simply "Let people love you," a message I hear repeatedly in recent days.

No other details. It's unsettling. What does it mean? Ruminating on it through the next several hours, I recognize it as an important message from my unconscious. Yet still I am frozen in silence.

I talk to Alan over coffee in the morning. What does he think it means?

"It sounds like you're saying it's your fault if you don't," he suggests.

"Well, it's true. I cut myself off from everyone. Even Carol. Do you ever feel like I keep myself from you?" I ask, and he says "I do at times."

Then he tells me that lately I've been caught up full time with my writing and other work. And if I'm not working, I'm shopping for the girls—buying uniforms for Cassidy, ski pants for Elodie. And a new dining table and towels for the house. Sometimes he's not sure where he fits in.

"But you're the most important person in my life. You, David, and the girls," I explain, distressed.

"Well, you're content to let me take care of most things—the shopping, the cooking. I often have to remind you to set the table."

What Alan says rings true. I get carried away, and I don't want him to feel neglected. I do most of the cooking in East Hampton, but in Brooklyn he carries more than his weight.

I'm amazed and grateful that we're having this conversation, that there's no edge in his voice, no sarcasm or slip into anger or criticism, and no defensiveness and shouting from me. We agree that we need to be more careful with each other, more aware of our care for each other. More affection. More kissing, and definitely more hugs!

"I'm sorry for taking you for granted," I admit.

"That's good," he says, smiling.

And that's that. We get back to our morning coffee, discussing goodies we'll want for our upcoming weekend with David and our girls.

But later that day and during those that followed, I obsess over what he said about neglect and my self-involvement. I'm less depressed than I was months ago when I was more debilitated from COVID. I am strong enough now to be his full partner. He has a right to one. I consciously assign responsibilities to both of us, and put our homes at the top of my daily focus list. I will do my share.

I have never known us to argue so peacefully. In the past, it was our way for him to become critical and dismissive and for me to lose my temper and become defensive, though that has subsided considerably over the years. We used to stay angry after a fight. Not so anymore. We get upset, voice it, snap back and forth once or twice, and drop it. No belaboring the point. No seemingly endless smoldering. This too is aging. Wisdom takes time. And this wasn't a fight. We had a discussion.

ANOTHER FISSURE

2020

A YEAR BEFORE MY DEPRESSION BEGAN TO EASE, DAVID AND Marlene separated. It was a long time coming, but she finally secured an apartment and moved out. They planned to share custody of Cassidy and Elodie, and due to the impeccable care that David and Marlene took in assuring the girls that they would remain the focus and treasure of their parents, they all handled it quite well. They settled into a new life. Alan and I were doubly grateful that we moved to Brooklyn so that we could be more present for them. Whatever fissure brought David and Marlene to this place in their marriage, they were as connected and committed as parents as one could dream of. This was a sad time, but the story was theirs to discuss or not with whomever they chose.

Rather than obsess on the pain of their lives, I chose music—a Brahms violin concerto—to listen to and feel. Brahms has always opened the wound in my chest with his minor tones: violins, cellos, horns.

Music, like my ocean, takes me where I need to go. Makes me face the pain—experience its texture, rhythm—each thin thread twisting and turning in its own tapestry of survival. The notes create the map that takes me through this steady current of loss to the other side and resolution, if only for an hour, a day. It's genuine work, battling with the depressive dark and the scream that's caught in my chest.

Where did the pain come from?

In my early teens, the teasing. In my thirties, my back. And then, Therapist Joan gently adds:

David and Marlene, Catherine, your aging body, COVID, racism, police brutality.

I wanted it to go away. Was I praying?

It's true. I often find myself praying with the vigor and faith that protected me as a child. It's like riding a bike. The impulse remains unconscious until the situation triggers it. I found solace in the fact that remnants of faith still lived in me. God, the Blessed Mother, Jesus, but also my caregivers, and confidantes—like Henny, Mom, Dad, and Catherine—were still there at the core. I suddenly recalled that I might be wrong in dismissing the whole holy universe I once so firmly believed in. Perhaps God exists. And if I was wrong in my loosening of faith, would I be damned? Like Judas?

But maybe Judas wasn't damned. Maybe God didn't turn His back on him or hurl him into Hell but rather, regarded his sin, his denial of Christ, as a flaw—a human flaw that, though tragic, did not erase the rest of his life. Maybe he was a decent man otherwise. Maybe he had children and parents and cared for them deeply. It goes back to my belief in a compassionate Jesus. The Jesus I loved didn't expect Judas to be perfect. Like he never expected me to be perfect. So, he wouldn't reject me. He'd know my heart, and He'd understand that I'm doing the best I can—I'm a good person whose values didn't change just because I stopped believing (did I?). And so, the process continued to spiral, and I was left with my original sense of a loving God who, if I'd been wrong and He really did exist, didn't turn away from me, but continued to trust the honesty of my intentions. I still belonged to Him. He would make room for me.

In the end I was safe. God was my Good Father. He forgave weakness (if that is what my lack of faith stems from), and He saw my commitment to lead a good and honest life. I still followed His guidelines. And if He existed, He was merciful. Even accepting my prayer. This was the God I grew up on. It was comforting to know He was still there.

If He was.

This was how my mind worked. I obsessed over an issue until I moved my way through all the steps to closure. The why. But then, in some cases, doubt followed assurance, and I was back to square one—vacillating again. And so, it continued.

Human behavior was and is my subject matter. It fascinated me all my life. Interestingly enough, I didn't refer to it as my career choice. It was more than that. A vocation really. Since I was a young girl, I needed to understand the psychology behind my own actions and those of others. It was part of my DNA and propelled inquiry, which is what created this memoir.

It reminded me of my struggle with COVID's acceleration in so many states. I asked Alan how it was possible that all these people saw the statistics and, in fact, probably knew people in their own circles who were infected and perhaps had died from the virus, and still they attended huge gatherings and rallies. They crowded beaches, refused to wear masks, and would not keep social distance. They even attended COVID parties! Why did they court the virus? To prove it didn't exist?

They were impervious to all attempts to convince them that this was real, that danger lurked. Did they not believe that? Were they so convinced that they were invulnerable? I wanted to understand, but I couldn't. Half of the country was psychotic, delusional. It was petrifying. And it was real!

Alan had no answer either. He was as troubled about this as I was.

X-RAYS & SCANS, PAST & PRESENT

2021

Alan and I are finally visiting Dr. O'Leary this morning. He's moved further uptown, but his office is still on Park Avenue. Despite my trepidation, I'm happy to see him. He appears no older than when I last visited his office except for more silver speckles at his temples. I stifle my impulse to ask what transpired, resulting in the move, and assume he has chosen a more modest office and is reducing his practice. Perhaps he's slowing down too.

That part scares me. Is he about to retire? He calms my nerves by mentioning that he's only moved in in the past few weeks, since quarantine has been lifted. That's encouraging. He must plan to be around for a while. He is seated at his mahogany desk and ten to twelve x-rays and scans, past and current, are displayed on a six-foot square monitor beside him. They are harder to make sense of today. I certainly don't want to see them. My heart is banging in my chest, but I begin by reviewing our plan to meet annually to assess my back. Though of course that was interrupted by COVID, and it's been two years, we are back on track. I express my concern about changes since my last appointment, then blurt out, "Will I end up in a wheelchair?" The question stuns all three of us.

"What makes you ask that?" he gently asks.

I tell him that it's what I've always been afraid of. I explain that I was told by one of the scoliosis surgeons that without fusion I'd need a wheelchair. After seeing my scans in our last visit, I was afraid that even though I had fusion, I would still need a chair.

"No indeed, you will not need a wheelchair. There are a few very slight changes noted on the most current scans but nothing of concern. Your back looks virtually the same as last time. You're doing just fine. You look well, and I'm glad to know that you're walking every day. I think our plan of you checking in every year or two is a good one. Pain is the most important barometer of your condition. And you have none. That's good news. Go enjoy yourself."

Relieved and on the edge of tears, I thank him and promise to return in another year, and just as I'm about to reach over and give him a kiss on the cheek, I remember COVID and offer him an elbow instead.

It takes me several weeks to cautiously, but deliberately, accept the great news. I repeat it over and over, "You're doing just fine . . . very slight changes . . . You won't need a wheelchair." Life-giving words.

POSSESSED

Ongoing

DURING MY MOTHER'S FINAL YEAR, I STARTED TO TAPE MY conversations with my parents. I was aware that their time was limited and that I knew very little about their individual family histories as well as the details of my mother's and father's lives. Mom's past was particularly mysterious. I became vigilant, carrying a small tape recorder whenever we were together, as my good friend Karen suggested. They grew accustomed to the recorder and soon became comfortable speaking as if it wasn't there. They both were present during most of our recorded conversations and each talked freely. Until then, Mom had refused to speak about her mother. When she saw how comfortable Dad was in sharing his stories, she opened up. I filled several CDs with their reminiscences and viewed them as holy work (prayers almost) that brought us closer. It's a practice that I recommend to others. All too often these stories die with our loved ones, and families are left with very aborted information about who their parents were before they became parents. I wanted to know as much as they were willing to share. And I wanted David to know about them too, as well as his girls, Alan, and my siblings.

As time passed, our cocoon became a safe place for the three of us. Sometimes the conversations took place on our shaded East Hampton deck in the summertime over late morning tea. But usually, my parents shared their stories as we sat at their dining table in Edgewater, enjoying lunches of Mom's famous tuna fish sandwiches and hefty mugs of tea. I asked them questions. Why did you come to America? Were your parents supportive? I can't imagine moving to the other side of the world and not seeing my siblings and parents. What was life like after your mother died? There were six of you and your dad; what role did you play in tending to the family? Dad, what was your relationship with your father? There were scores of questions from me and ready answers from them that they often elaborated on. They were clearly enjoying this return to their earlier lives and seemed grateful to share their stories.

After a lifetime of silence, Mom shared her mother with us. Eventually, I transcribed their stories and turned them into poems that became the bedrock of my verse memoir, *Orphans*. My parents' language was so melodic that it fit gracefully into couplets.

Her life would be in danger if she had any more children,
the doctor'd said. But what was she to do?

If the Lord decided to send you another,
that's just the way it was.

I watched through a crack in the door, trembling
at the sight of her writhing in the bed.

The pastor arrived to give her last rites,
but I kept pleading with the Lord to let her live.

But He didn't answer.
I guess He just wanted her with Him.

"Siobhan . . . Siobhan . . . ," the women whispered
as the writhing slowed and wailing gave way

to forced breath. Then her eyes popped
wide like something had scared her.

The doctor crept closer and closed them.
"Lord, have mercy on her departed soul,"

he pronounced, and the women began
to wash her. "But maybe she's not dead!"

I screamed silently. "Please, Jesus, please . . ."
Then they were combing her hair.

She had beautiful long red hair.
I still see her laid out on the bed

in a long brown habit like a sister
would wear, or a monk.

I crawled close to the bed,
crouching beside her on the floor;

tassels from her habit hung over me.
Nobody knew I was there.

I was six.

•

It was something awful, it was—
our mother dying.

There were six of us kids and our father
left behind. After the funeral, we went

back home and picked up our lives.
I watched Baby Dan while my father

tended the cattle. And the others went
to school. I finally got to go too

when my father took Dan on his back
as he farmed. But the life was gone

from him and grief scarred his face.
Yet he never spoke of her again.

No one did. It was terrible.
Like she never lived at all.

•

Dan and I were always together:
I was his mother, and I loved

having my own child. As he grew up,
he followed after me wherever I went.

The others left us alone. So, I
made my own home. Just me and Dan.

But there was a darkness in him,
a sadness. Nothing we talked about

(you didn't talk much back then), but
I could see it. Then one day, he was

barely twelve, he was gone. We searched
everywhere, but he was nowhere to be found.

We knew he'd run away. It was terrible living,
knowing our mom died giving birth to him.

I prayed hard to my mother
in the hopes she'd help me find him.

But she didn't.
He showed up at Jim's in Leicester

when he was an old man and about to die.
That was four years ago when Dad and

I went back to see him. Didn't have much
to say. Then he was gone again.

We got word later that he'd died
of a cancer in a hospital in London.

First, I lost my mother,
then Dan,

but I kept them in my heart
all these years.

I was shattered when I heard Mom's story. How did she live watching her mother die? How did she sit around the dinner table with her dad and siblings talking about ordinary things—the cow getting ready to calf, the bitter cold, the potatoes in short supply with no mention of their deceased mother (not then, not ever—it was as if she never lived,

Mom had said)? How does one survive such pain—first, her mother, then her brother. My chest heaves with the fire of that loss.

What I came to understand through the stories is that Dad had a splendid mother and Mom did not. Dad's sisters, my Aunts Rose, May, and Peg, visited our family a lot and, unlike Dad, they were lusty talkers, discussing the sibling relationships, and enthusiastically telling us tales about their beloved mother, Catherine. My grandmother was an icon in their eyes—a schoolteacher, mother of nine, an ebullient conversationalist, fancy dresser, fine cook, and storyteller. She also found the time to tend the farm with my grandfather and sew clothes for herself and all her children. Clearly, she adored them, and they adored their larger-than-life mother. Mom's mother, on the other hand, was a topic we knew not to ask about. Aunt Eileen, the only one of Mom's sisters we knew—though we were aware of Margaret, who still lived in Ireland—never mentioned their mother either. I can only imagine Mom's longing when she heard about the feats and adventures of Dad's amazing mother. And she was still alive!

Catherine was the first child born to Mom and Dad and was named after Dad's mother. All my father's relatives said she looked like her grandmother as well. Recently I've come up with a possible explanation for Mom's rejection of Catherine. I think it's rooted in our names. Lately, I've been wondering how that naming decision was made. Was it a collaborative choice of the two of them? I don't think Dad would have insisted, and Mom probably assumed it was the obvious choice. Memories of her own mother were carefully tucked away, hidden inside her. During one of our taped conversations, Mom confided that she had been her mother's favorite child.

"We were very much alike," she said. "We both loved clothes and Mammy made sure I had lots of them." Interesting how stories repeat across generations.

The thought that her mother was absent breaks my heart for the lonely child, lonely adult Mom. According to her, Dad's sisters indulged Catherine, the miracle baby and their mother's namesake, stepping over each other to play with their beautiful niece, first child of their favorite brother. Two years later, Sonny came—the miraculous boy named for our father (Eugene). Mom confided that just as my aunts took over when Catherine was born, they did the same thing when Sonny arrived.

"I was left to do the cleaning and cooking while they played with the babies," Mom complained.

But soon she was pregnant again, and eleven months after Sonny's arrival, I was born. This child was entirely hers. She named me Joan, after her mother, Siobhan.

"And I never let anyone near you," she proudly confided.

My mother finally had a replacement for the adored mother she had lost when she was six years old.

The fourth child in our clan was Jerry, named for Mom's brother. I suppose Jerry was Mom's too. What did it mean to be hers? Did she love us more? I think she had no choice.

I suffered lifelong guilt about our mother's favoritism of me over Catherine. All she heard was "Joan is so beautiful and smart; look at her hair, thick and wavy; she does so well in school; she's a model in these clothes." It was endless. It seemed to follow that it all had to do with our names.

PREORDAINED

2022

THE EXPLORATION OF MY LIFE CONTINUES. THOUGH I'VE SPENT plenty of time blaming Mom for rejecting Catherine, I no longer believe that it was meanness on Mom's part. Nor was it simply a function of Mom's jealousy that Dad and Catherine were so close. My focus on their troubled mother–daughter relationship thus far leads me to the conclusion that Mom's resentment was preordained. For all practical purposes, Catherine was taken from her by my father's sisters. Just as her mother was taken from her and later her beloved brother, Dan, who disappeared when he was twelve years old.

When, amazingly, Dan and my mother met forty years later in London, he admitted that he couldn't bear living with the thought that he was the cause of their mother's death. He was convinced that everyone blamed him. Such loss for him and for Mom, who couldn't bear losing yet another love.

Contrary to the Mom who demonstrated significant ambivalence as Catherine grew, that didn't seem to be evident when Cath was an infant. I have several pictures of Mom smiling at her beautiful baby Catherine, with her shock of black hair, dressed in hat, sweater, and booties Mom crocheted herself.

"Different outfits for every day," she declared proudly. "Pink, yellow, green, every color but blue, of course. Women would stop me in the park as I wheeled Catherine in the carriage and ask if they could pay me to make outfits for their babies. But I said no. I had no time. Besides, these were special for Catherine. And because Catherine was a neat baby, she never got dirty," Mom bragged. "She was as clean when I took her clothes off as she was when I put them on. Not like you, always playing in the dirt," she laughed (comments tinged with sarcasm were typical of my mother).

But it was hard understanding the reason for Mom's preference for me. It plagued me. As my sister grew up, Mom fixed her special foods when the rest of us were having something that Catherine didn't like. Which was Mom's way. I recall many mornings when she made different breakfasts for two or three of us: banana eggnog for Sonny, pancakes for Catherine, and Wheatena for Jerry and me. I remember her sewing skirts for Catherine and me, and complaining that while I wore them, Catherine didn't want to. She liked to wear only the clothes she shopped for with her friends.

When Catherine was thirteen years old, she became convinced that she was adopted and that that was the reason for Mom's rejection. She was always searching the house for adoption papers. It was clear to all of us that she felt unloved and didn't fit in, even though she looked just like Dad's mother. Eventually, she confronted Mom about this. Perhaps this made Mom feel rejected too. Catherine confided in her friends, not Mom. Maybe Mom felt that she didn't measure up next to them? Theirs was a very sad story. One reflecting the elaborate tapestry that was woven for them by life circumstances beyond their understanding or control.

Slowly I take this in. I'm aware of having resolved a puzzle that I've repressed most of my adult life. A quiet joy comes with it. As does relief. My writing releases memories.

WHEN THE WATER IS THERE

2022

WITH COVID QUARANTINE FINISHED, WE'RE FINALLY ABLE TO come out of our houses and apartments. There seems to be a spring in everyone's step. Yesterday Alan and I received another booster shot. The report from the CDC cautions us to continue wearing our masks. The virus is still out there though in lesser degrees.

We're all so happy to have a reprieve from the isolation of the past many months and celebrate by getting in the car and going to the Bay. Once there, David and the girls fly down to the water. Cassidy spins, enchanted in her maxi dress. Pink and turquoise gauze lifts gracefully with the breeze. Elodie and David are at water's edge, the wind is picking up. I am safe on a teak bench above the beach. My inclination is to criticize my fear of walking the rocky stretch to join them, especially as I watch an agile and fearless gray-headed woman, clearly my age, making her way effortlessly down the path. But I refuse my put-down. *Refocus!* I insist.

There is such joy in the viewing. I am here with them at a distance. They know that. And I have been here before—many injuries ago—sitting on this bench while David, a small boy, played in the sand with his dad. I remind myself that there is no crime in being careful. It is not a shame to watch rather than actively participate. Cassidy accepts the fact that some places are too rocky for Grandma to walk. After a brief respite, she's spinning again, then plops onto the sand with her father and sister. I remember so many days when David was a child and we made our way down to the beach and the water, hunted marbleized stones and shells, had picnics sitting on the largest rocks then feasted on peanut butter and jelly sandwiches and grapes, his favorites. I was nimbler thirty-five years ago, before my back and ankle fusions. Now, David reminds me of how I used to write at the beach. We both found inspiration here, at one time or another. He doesn't understand why I stopped coming to this spot, especially when I was struggling with my writing. I wonder too. I know I would have missed him—I always picture us together at the Bay. I don't think of coming here alone. Maybe I should.

With evening coming, after our family beach outing, I go for an evening walk and find a spot on the pier close to the place where the water hits the pilings and the seaweed-wrapped rocks. The sound sends me back to my girlhood home, living a block from the beach. Gentle, reassuring, the movement of the water has always been a lullaby for me. Particularly on those evenings when I returned to the beach—empty of other people—and sat at the edge of the bulkhead, listening to the music of the waves. Just me and the water. I wasn't rushing then. I had patience. Tonight, I also have patience. I just sit with the waning tide.

SELF-PARENTING

2022 / Ongoing

I'M NOTICING A PEACEFUL QUIET LATELY. LESS ANXIETY, SIGNIFICANTLY less depression. How did they abate? I ask myself.

Therapist Joan answers:

> First and foremost, I listen to your anxiety. It's not a surprise that you become frightened when some new issue arises. That you need to be reassured for a good while before you can begin to get perspective. It has to do with control and self-nurturing.

In the past, my tendency has been not to trust the concept of control. I've seen it as defensive, antifeeling. Anti-therapeutic. What I've learned during these last two years is that control can be a very positive force in my efforts to encourage my mental health. Just as I must actively exercise my body to stay strong physically, I have to exercise my mind and heart to be mentally strong.

There comes a time in the therapeutic relationship when the "aha-moments" significantly diminish. That is as it should be. Treatment up until then involves exploration of everyday stressors as well as emotional and psychological issues that trouble us. That time is rich with discovery and involves a "letting go" of control—relaxing the defenses that are no longer working because they are outdated and unnecessary due to a change in circumstances. The next phase is the toughest—the working through, whereby the work involves putting what has been learned into practice. And practice is the right word. It implies repetition. Not mastery! It involves doing the same thing over and over to retrain the psyche and the body. The goal is to change behavior. This process requires going through day-to-day life and relationships, identifying places in which specific unconscious behaviors have become repetitious and crop up without awareness. These are indicators of yet another defensive response—repetition compulsion. The impulse to do the same thing over and over irrespective of results.

How do I break the patterns? By steadfast observation of my behavior and my analysis of what works and what doesn't. By repeatedly reminding myself of the fact that I am not victim to these compulsions but can elect to change them. This is the homework of therapy—watching and catching myself as I keep walking into the same wall. I must relentlessly confront myself with what I'm doing. Then decide to change that behavior in the hope of a better outcome. This is tough, frustrating work. Eliminating a behavior that has become a habit takes time. I become furious with my therapist self and the process.

This is what I refer to as the "Come to Jesus Meeting." It's time to take myself in line. Become increasingly more vigilant in observing myself. Insist that I take care of myself. Refuse to give in to the part of me that doesn't want to walk, the me that wants to fall apart in self-pity, seeing myself as unable or disabled, wimpy, out in the cold without my coat. Old.

This is the process of self-parenting. Caring for myself as I did David—insisting on healthy behaviors, settings, relationships. Making demands on myself, but only if the demands are reasonable and doable. Even for those in traditional therapy, waiting to change, not taking the next step until one is emotionally ready, takes a very long time. I know what I have to do. So, I use that. When crisis hits, I'm inclined to be anxious, to revert to behaviors that I know don't work. That's a danger time. There is comfort in what's known and reverting to familiar (albeit unhealthy) behavior. In my case, I often doubt my ability to handle a problem. But I can't give up. Nor do I have the right to beat myself up.

When I start leveling accusations at myself, which I know only deepens self-hatred, I refuse to accept the self-assault. Right down to shouting at myself—and yes, I do mean out loud shouting—*F*** OFF!* I must actively try to defend myself against the me that's ready to feel weak, unworthy.

I'm aware of a strength that I haven't had for years. Or never had. There is no way that I could have felt and demonstrated such self-care before this. I'm becoming a loving parent to myself, relentless as my mother was all those years ago, insisting that my height was something to be proud of. Taking the reins and trusting my impulses like I trusted my decision to leave the Church so long ago. This is a clear signal for me that the depression is lifting.

Sunset at the Bay. This amazing place murmurs the same rippling-water sound as it meets the beach that I experienced during my girlhood evenings. It brings me back to the regenerating music of the water that I loved as a child. It was so lovely to have rekindled my love for the water a few weeks ago on the pier by our apartment in Brooklyn. Now here it is again in East Hampton, where it's been waiting all these years. I thought recently that this is the sound I would want to soothe me when I'm dying. To me, this isn't morbid. In fact, it is comforting, reassuring. When the water is present, I'm not alone. Or afraid.

A BIRTHDAY PICNIC

2022

IT'S OCTOBER. THE SUN IS TAKING A BREATHER. NOT GONE, BUT gentle, firing up every once in a while when I'm missing it and knowing enough to tuck back into itself when I need some rest. Today, I'm collecting gifts—a more natural impulse lately as I make my way through the depression that spiraled through Catherine's illness and death and my ever-increasing physical vulnerability. This morning Cassidy and Elodie woke Pop-Pop and me for an early morning picnic in bed and a Tinker Bell movie. David served hot chocolates as all of us cuddled in one lump of delicious giggling and tickling. What a way to begin a birthday! It's my eighty-first!

After our dinner, Cassidy finishes off as much broccoli as she can stuff in her mouth and leaves the table to wander around the dining room. She picks up various decorative pieces and studies them. Uncannily, she always selects my favorites—crystal candlesticks, etched silver, the Waterford hurricane lamp. Tonight, it's the French hand-painted wine decanter—thin and delicate as a seashell, and just as vulnerable.

"What's this, Grandma?" she asks, while gently removing it from its place on the carved teak pedestal just as her father jumps in to protect it.

"She knows how to touch it," I say.

"What is it?" she asks.

"It's a vessel for wine," I answer. "Like the white pitcher is for water. It was painted by an artist who lived many years ago. You know how much you love to paint? Well, this person did too, and she made it her life's work. My favorite parts are the long, thin neck and brilliant royal and magenta colors."

She asks where it came from, and I explain that I found it at an antique shop, "where you can see whole rooms filled with delicate pieces made by hand. Like silver knives and forks with pearl curlicue handles and hand-painted dishes, rings, necklaces, and lots of beautiful dresses that ladies wore a hundred years ago. We'll visit one together the next time we're here."

"Yay! Yay!" from Cass, as Elodie, her chorus, shouts, "Me too, me too!"

AS LONG AS THERE'S A NEEDLE HOLDING ON

2022

One of the great things about aging (and I can't believe I'm saying this) is the slow pace that comes with it. Time opens like a valise filled with details of lives and events I've only known superficially. Now my perceptions are deeper, with thousands of nuances I did not put together until this year, as I was sitting in my fuchsia robe on my cozy chair in the middle of any given afternoon. I've retired into a life doing what I love best—writing, hanging out with Alan, David, and our girls. The act of writing this book has deepened my relationships with the living and the dead. Particularly with my mother. And Catherine. Focusing on the intimacy I shared with both before they died. Putting together the puzzle of Catherine, me, Mom. Thinking about my grandmother Catherine in a new way, and my mother's mother, Siobhan. All of this required an openness and courage that allowed me to reach this psychological place. Though I'm a speculative person and a competent psychologist, it never occurred to me that answers were waiting—as simply and closely as having the time and place in my life to pay attention and ask the questions. To probe deeply by writing. To learn by writing.

Remarkably, this tall girl is growing. That's the glory. Along the way, I've discovered the secret of aging is knowing and understanding the life I've lived. Through memories. And time. When I started this journey, time was rushing. Of late, it seems to have slowed, as I have. My life is simplified to just what I most love. I am gratefully reaching wellness, like the magnificent blue spruce with its eager, high branches throwing rich blue fronds skyward.

Coda

HUMAN

2021 / Ongoing

I RECALL COMING TO A SECTION OF A CHEKHOV STORY WHEREIN THE protagonist was exploring his emotional connection to a lover. Along with love, admiration, and passion, he also felt hatred. My gut reaction was to argue with Chekhov, accuse him of overdramatizing and overstating these emotions. Hatred? Anger was more appropriate. But the longer I thought about it and examined my own impulses, the more convinced I was that Chekhov was right. Hatred can be part of love.

As I look back on my relationship with Alan and those closest to me, I must admit to anger thickening to hate even at the center of love. At times, I have hated loved ones—my mother, my three siblings, even Alan and my father—when they've trodden on my most basic needs for acceptance or love or when they've betrayed my trust. Love is vulnerable and fragile. It can be wounded and it can wound. We tend to think of hate as irrevocable, all pervasive, enduring, and arresting, wiping out all other feelings. But hate can be temporary—in fact, it is often short-lived and confined to a specific event or time. These are nuances that many people would refute—you can't love and hate someone at the same time. But we can and we do. The great writers knew that.

How blessed am I (are we!) to come upon a character who, in the depths of their soul, reflects my own tendency to hate, to be envious, self-serving, greedy, or any one of the many feelings that so shame me that I try to keep hidden from myself and the world. There's permission in that. If I can forgive these feelings in others, perhaps I can forgive them in myself.

This is something I feel very deeply—a part of my humanity that I often reject. My wish to be my idealized self sends me spinning into a life of denial and rejection of all but the most generous and laudatory emotions. The challenge to be honest and open with myself is ever-present and unrelenting. I've come a long way in opening up to my own underbelly. But the road is long—it's perhaps the most urgent and profound challenge of my life—and I owe it to the person I want to be and know I can become.

Here, there is truth and wisdom, forgiveness and opportunity for growth. Accepting the existence of my faults frees me to monitor my behavior and impulses and to work to transform my shortcomings into a means of self-improvement. That challenge is my life's work. I can't be perfect—no human is—but I can do better if I choose to. No matter how old I am. That is the level of control I *actually* have as a human being. We all do.

GRATITUDES

We often hear "It takes a village." Blessed with a community that has tended to the growth and health of my beloved *Lights in Cold Rooms* from its inception, I wholeheartedly agree. My village has been there through the entire process of birthing this book, and I'm so grateful to celebrate her entry into the world together. Each has left their imprint on the life we have created together. Thank you! Thank you, my dear ones!

First and foremost are my two families: my first being my beloved husband, Alan, and our son, David, whose belief in me has never wavered. David's daughters, Cassidy and Elodie have infused more light into our lives than we could ever have imagined.

Beside the Handlers in this banquet are the amazing and devoted family of CavanKerry Press, Gabriel Cleveland, Dimitri Reyes, Dana Harris-Trovato, and Tamara Al-Qaisi-Coleman, whose publishing skills produced the body of the book that *Lights* has become.

Assisting Gabe in his loving attention to *Lights* is Mike Corrao, creator of the striking and imaginative cover and interior design who still made time to indulge my obsessions over each decision we made. Editor Jan Freeman and copy editors Joy Arbor and Bridget Reaume provided expert counsel as we worked to dress *Lights* in her finest clothes.

Abundant gratitude to my loving girlfriends Teresa Carson, Karen Chase, Carol Snyder, and niece Aimeé Helmaniak, who read *Lights* in its many iterations (as well as all my other books), offering wise and perceptive feedback and generous support.

Throughout my entire writing life, I have been graced with the friendship, mentorship, and editorial care of Molly Peacock and Baron Wormser, who have taught me what I know about poems and the writing of them and have encouraged me to trust my own voice—their comments about *Lights* are a reflection of their belief in me.

Thank you! Bless you, my loving village!

CAVANKERRY'S MISSION

A not-for-profit literary press serving art and community, CavanKerry is committed to expanding the reach of poetry and other fine literature to a general readership by publishing works that explore the emotional and psychological landscapes of everyday life, and to bringing that art to the underserved where they live, work, and receive services.

OTHER BOOKS IN THE NOTABLE VOICES SERIES

The Lost Nostalgias, Esteban Rodriguez
All at Once, Jack Ridl
Glitter Road, by January Gill O'Neil
Limited Editions, Carole Stone
Deep Are These Distances Between Us, Susan Atefat-Peckham
The History Hotel, Baron Wormser
Dialect of Distant Harbors, Dipika Mukherjee
The Snow's Wife, Frannie Lindsay
Eleanor, Gray Jacobik
Without My Asking, Robert Cording
Miss August, Nin Andrews
A Car Stops and a Door Opens, Christopher Bursk
Letters from Limbo, Jeanne Marie Beaumont
Tornadoesque, Donald Platt
Only So Far, Robert Cording
Unidentified Sighing Objects, Baron Wormser
How They Fell, Annie Boutelle
The Bar of the Flattened Heart, David Keller
Same Old Story, Dawn Potter
The Laundress Catches Her Breath, Paola Corso
American Rhapsody, Carole Stone
Impenitent Notes, Baron Wormser
Walking with Ruskin, Robert Cording
Divina Is Divina, Jack Wiler
How the Crimes Happened, Dawn Potter
Descent, John Haines
Southern Comfort, Nin Andrews
Losing Season, Jack Ridl

Without Wings, Laurie Lamon

An Apron Full of Beans: New and Selected Poems, Sam Cornish

The Poetry Life: Ten Stories, Baron Wormser

BEAR, Karen Chase

Fun Being Me, Jack Wiler

Common Life, Robert Cording

The Origins of Tragedy & Other Poems, Kenneth Rosen

Apparition Hill, Mary Ruefle

Against Consolation, Robert Cording

This book was printed on paper from responsible sources.

Lights in Cold Rooms was typeset in Freight Sans,
created in 2005 by Joshua Darden as part of the Freight Collection,
which includes a vast array of utilitarian typefaces.